普通高等学校旅游管理教材

酒店商务英语
（第 2 版）

主　编　唐　羽　韩　笑
副主编　邢　舫　冷婧超

清华大学出版社
北京交通大学出版社
·北京·

内容简介

本书为旅游酒店管理专业系列教材之一，共分为十个单元，配有五套综合模拟测试练习题。每个单元由"学习目标、背景知识、对话训练、快速阅读、写作技巧、词汇扩展"等部分组成。每个单元一个主题，涵盖听、说、读、写、练等基本环节。本书侧重于现代酒店重要构成部门的服务用语及酒店业相关内容，包括预订服务、入住服务、客房服务、餐饮服务、宴会服务、通信服务、会议服务、休闲娱乐服务、退房服务及应对特殊问题等内容。

本书构思新颖，内容独特，实用性强，使用范围广，适合普通高等院校、应用型本科及高职高专院校的酒店管理专业教学使用，同时可用作酒店业服务与管理人员的培训教材，也可作为酒店从业人员自学的书籍。

本书封面贴有清华大学出版社防伪标签，无标签者不得销售。
版权所有，侵权必究。侵权举报电话：010-62782989　13501256678　13801310933

图书在版编目（CIP）数据

酒店商务英语 / 唐羽，韩笑主编. —2版. —北京：北京交通大学出版社：清华大学出版社，2021.4
（普通高等学校旅游管理教材）
ISBN 978-7-5121-4442-2

Ⅰ. ①酒… Ⅱ. ①唐… ②韩… Ⅲ. ①饭店-商务-英语-教材 Ⅳ. ①F719.2

中国版本图书馆CIP数据核字（2021）第060918号

酒店商务英语
JIUDIAN SHANGWU YINGYU

责任编辑：吴嫦娥
出版发行：清华大学出版社　邮编：100084　电话：010-62776969　http://www.tup.com.cn
　　　　　北京交通大学出版社　邮编：100044　电话：010-51686414　http://www.bjtup.com.cn
印　刷　者：北京时代华都印刷有限公司
经　　销：全国新华书店
开　　本：185 mm×260 mm　印张：11.25　字数：281千字
版 印 次：2016年9月第1版　2021年4月第2版　2021年4月第1次印刷
定　　价：39.00元

本书如有质量问题，请向北京交通大学出版社质监组反映。对您的意见和批评，我们表示欢迎和感谢。
投诉电话：010-51686043，51686008；传真：010-62225406；E-mail：press@bjtu.edu.cn。

前言

酒店商务英语是普通高等院校、高等职业及专科学校、成人教育酒店管理专业的一门核心课程。通过"听、说、读、写"四位一体的教学模式，使学生能很好地掌握酒店管理专业基本的理论知识，并将英语更恰当地运用于酒店管理与服务的过程中。

随着中国酒店业的迅速发展，我国将成为世界第一大旅游接待国。为了适应我国旅游业的蓬勃发展，适应世界第一大旅游市场的人才需要，我国各大专院校急需培养出既有酒店管理专业知识基础又能够自如运用英语对客服务与交流的复合型人才。因此，增强酒店专业英语教学具有重要的现实意义。

本书以"单元"为基本结构形式，将教学内容分解为若干个训练部分，向读者提供比较全面的学习及练习指导材料，并突出三大特色。

第一，实用性强。在编写过程中坚持实用性原则，专业知识通俗易懂，突出实际英语训练环节，重点加强对学生英语服务技能的培养与训练。

第二，可理解性强。本书语言简练，主要运用酒店各场合实际情景模拟教学，使读者能够模仿真实环境进行学习与训练。

第三，针对性强。围绕酒店英语服务技能的内容和要求，着眼于酒店各部门的英语服务训练，突出较强的专业性。

本书由唐羽（辽宁科技学院）、韩笑（本溪市商贸服务学校）担任主编，邢舫（沈阳工学院）、冷婧超（辽宁科技学院）担任副主编。本书编写人员结合酒店业市场的发展和职业服务的技能需要，突出体现"课程结构职业化、实际操作模块化、顶岗实习标准化"的应用型教学模式。

本书在编写过程中，参考了大量资料，部分来源于互联网和编写组成员日常的教学积累资料，有些资料无法核实准确出处，在此一并向相关单位和作者表示感谢！编者水平所限，书中疏漏和不足之处在所难免，恳请专家与读者批评指正！

本书配有教学课件及习题答案，需求者可发邮件至 183681911@qq.com 索取。

编者

2021 年 5 月

目录 Contents

Unit 1　Reservation Service 预订服务 ·· 1
　Learning objectives 学习目标 ·· 1
　Part 1　Background knowledge 背景知识 ·· 1
　Part 2　Speaking 对话训练 ·· 2
　Part 3　Reading 快速阅读 ·· 6
　Part 4　Writing 写作技巧 ·· 13
　Part 5　Vocabulary Expansion 词汇扩展 ·· 14

Unit 2　Check-in Service 入住服务 ·· 15
　Learning objectives 学习目标 ·· 15
　Part 1　Background knowledge 背景知识 ·· 15
　Part 2　Speaking 对话训练 ·· 17
　Part 3　Reading 快速阅读 ·· 20
　Part 4　Writing 写作技巧 ·· 25
　Part 5　Vocabulary Expansion 词汇扩展 ·· 26

Unit 3　Housekeeping Service 客房服务 ·· 28
　Learning objectives 学习目标 ·· 28
　Part 1　Background knowledge 背景知识 ·· 28
　Part 2　Speaking 对话训练 ·· 31
　Part 3　Reading 快速阅读 ·· 34
　Part 4　Writing 写作技巧 ·· 39
　Part 5　Vocabulary Expansion 词汇扩展 ·· 40

Unit 4 Food & Beverage Service 餐饮服务 ·············· 42
   Learning objectives 学习目标 ························· 42
   Part 1　Background knowledge 背景知识 ··············· 42
   Part 2　Speaking 对话训练 ·························· 44
   Part 3　Reading 快速阅读 ·························· 50
   Part 4　Writing 写作技巧 ··························· 53
   Part 5　Vocabulary Expansion 词汇扩展 ················ 56

Unit 5 Banquet Service 宴会服务 ······················ 58
   Learning objectives 学习目标 ························· 58
   Part 1　Background knowledge 背景知识 ··············· 58
   Part 2　Speaking 对话训练 ·························· 59
   Part 3　Reading 快速阅读 ·························· 63
   Part 4　Writing 写作技巧 ··························· 69
   Part 5　Vocabulary Expansion 词汇扩展 ················ 70

Unit 6 Communication Service 通信服务 ················ 72
   Learning objectives 学习目标 ························· 72
   Part 1　Background knowledge 背景知识 ··············· 72
   Part 2　Speaking 对话训练 ·························· 73
   Part 3　Reading 快速阅读 ·························· 77
   Part 4　Writing 写作技巧 ··························· 83
   Part 5　Vocabulary Expansion 词汇扩展 ················ 84

Unit 7 Meeting Service 会议服务 ······················ 87
   Learning objectives 学习目标 ························· 87
   Part 1　Background knowledge 背景知识 ··············· 87
   Part 2　Speaking 对话训练 ·························· 89
   Part 3　Reading 快速阅读 ·························· 94
   Part 4　Writing 写作技巧 ··························· 101
   Part 5　Vocabulary Expansion 词汇扩展 ················ 102

Unit 8　Recreation and Entertainment 休闲娱乐服务 …………………… 104
　　Learning objectives 学习目标 ………………………………………………… 104
　　Part 1　Background knowledge 背景知识 ………………………………… 104
　　Part 2　Speaking 对话训练 ………………………………………………… 105
　　Part 3　Reading 快速阅读 ………………………………………………… 109
　　Part 4　Writing 写作技巧 ………………………………………………… 112
　　Part 5　Vocabulary Expansion 词汇扩展 ………………………………… 113

Unit 9　Check-out Service 退房服务 ……………………………………… 117
　　Learning objectives 学习目标 ………………………………………………… 117
　　Part 1　Background knowledge 背景知识 ………………………………… 117
　　Part 2　Speaking 对话训练 ………………………………………………… 119
　　Part 3　Reading 快速阅读 ………………………………………………… 122
　　Part 4　Writing 写作技巧 ………………………………………………… 129
　　Part 5　Vocabulary Expansion 词汇扩展 ………………………………… 131

Unit 10　Dealing With Special Problems 应对特殊问题 ………………… 133
　　Learning objectives 学习目标 ………………………………………………… 133
　　Part 1　Background knowledge 背景知识 ………………………………… 133
　　Part 2　Speaking 对话训练 ………………………………………………… 134
　　Part 3　Reading 快速阅读 ………………………………………………… 138
　　Part 4　Writing 写作技巧 ………………………………………………… 141
　　Part 5　Vocabulary Expansion 词汇扩展 ………………………………… 143

Test 1 ……………………………………………………………………………… 145
Test 2 ……………………………………………………………………………… 150
Test 3 ……………………………………………………………………………… 155
Test 4 ……………………………………………………………………………… 159
Test 5 ……………………………………………………………………………… 164

参考文献 …………………………………………………………………………… 171

Unit 1 Reservation Service 预订服务

Unit 1

Reservation Service 预订服务

Learning objectives 学习目标

After learning this unit, you should
- acquire the knowledge about how to reserve a hotel room;
- organize the basic words and expressions about reservation;
- learn some cultural knowledge about hotel reservation;
- find ways to improve your writing skills in reservation application forms;
- be familiar with some famous hotels at home and abroad.

 Part 1 Background knowledge 背景知识

Reservation is now widely adopted as a promotion method; meanwhile reservation makes it possible for the hotel to be well prepared as guests' requirements.

Reservation Methods 预订的方式

1. Telephone Reservation（电话预订）

Telephone reservation is quick, personal and convenient, therefore customers could adjust their schedules according to the information provided by the reception on the phone. Yet language may prove to be the main obstacle, such as foreign languages, dialects or even

1

weak voices during the phone call. To avoid mistakes, the clerk answering the call must write down reservation details carefully and repeat the information for the guest to confirm.

2. Fax Reservation（传真预订）

Fax reservation is more formal and accurate, which decreases mistakes and future disputes.

3. Internet Reservation（网络预订）

Internet reservation is the latest method that is used by an increasing number of people, as it is more convenient and inexpensive.

4. Mail Reservation（邮件预订）

Travel agency mainly makes use of mail reservation.

5. Oral Reservation（口头预订）

Oral reservation offers chances for a hotel to fully understand a guest's requirements as he will go personally or ask the agent to reserve in the hotel.

6. Contract Reservation（合约预订）

Contract reservation is usually in place for long-term renting with commercial cooperators or travel agencies.

Part 2　Speaking 对话训练

Dialogue 1

A Group Reservation

(Scene: A guest calls the hotel to reserve rooms for an American group.

R: Receptionist; G: Guest)

R: Shanghai Hotel, Reservation Desk. May I help you?

G: Yes, I'd like to make a group reservation in your hotel.

R: What kind of rooms would you like, sir? We have single rooms, twin rooms, double rooms, and deluxe suites in Chinese, Japanese, Roman, French and presidential styles.

G: We'd like to have 12 double rooms and a Japanese suite.

R: Oh, I see. May I have the name of the group?

Unit 1　Reservation Service 预订服务

G: The American Education Delegation.

R: For how many nights?

G: From May 23rd to May 27th, 4 nights in total.

R: May I have your name, sir?

G: George Smith.

R: Oh, I see. The American Education Delegation would like to have 12 double rooms and a Japanese suite from May 23rd to May 27th.

G: Thank you. Could you tell me how much you'll charge for a double room? And do you have a special rate for group reservations?

R: For one night, a double room in our hotel is 800 yuan and a Japanese suite is 1 200 yuan, we also offer a special rate for group reservations, a 20 percent discount. So, it's only 640 yuan for a double room and 960 yuan for a suite.

G: That's great. Could you pick us up at the airport?

R: Yes, of course. Our shuttle bus will be waiting for you at the airport. But could you give me the flight number, in case the flight is delayed?

G: MU435. And have you got a big conference hall? We'll have a meeting in your hotel during our stay in Shanghai.

R: Yes, sir. We have a very nice multi-media hall on the second floor. But I'm afraid you'll have to reserve it with the sales manager. Would you please hold on, and I'll check whether I can put you through.

G: That's fine. Thank you.

R: I'm always at your service.

Notes

1. deluxe　　　　　　　　　精装的，豪华的
2. delegation　　　　　　　代表团
3. special　　　　　　　　　特别的，特殊的，专门的
4. pick sb. up at the airport　去机场接某人，接机
5. shuttle bus　　　　　　　往返汽车，机场大巴
6. multi-media　　　　　　 多媒体的
7. put through　　　　　　 经受，测试；接通电话

Dialogue 2

Registering a Tour Group

(A: Tour group coordinator; B: Tour group guide; C: Leader of tour group)

A: Good evening. Who is the tour guide, please?

B: It's me.

A: Hello. My name is Wang Nan, the tour group coordinator. Welcome to our hotel. I'd like to reconfirm your reservation.

B: Hello. My name is Liu Ming, the tour guide. This is the leader of our tour group, Mr. Smith.

A: Nice to meet you.

B: Nice to meet you, too.

A: Is there any change in the number of your group members?

B: No.

A: Very good, sir. You have made a reservation for 12 double rooms and 4 single rooms. Here is the room list. Do you have a group visa?

C: Yes. Here you are.

A: All right. I'll get your group visa photocopied. Please wait a minute.

A: Here are the room cards and breakfast vouchers, Mr. Liu. Are you going to distribute them yourself?

B: No, I'll give them to Mr. Smith. He will distribute them.

A: May I confirm your check-out time? According to the schedule, you will check out at 8:00 a.m. on 18th, is it right?

B: I'm sorry that we'd like to change our check-out time to 8:30 a.m.

A: No problem, sir. What time would you like to have a morning call?

B: 7:00 a.m.

A: I see. 7:00 a.m. on 18th. Could you please place your luggage in front of your room doors by 8:00 a.m.? The bellman will pick them up. Anything else?

B: No. Thank you.

A: If there is any change, please inform the Front Desk.

B: OK. Thank you.

A: Thank you. Enjoy your stay.

酒店商务英语

Notes

1. visa	签证
2. get ... photocopied	复制，复印
3. voucher	凭证，收据
4. distribute	分发；分配；分布；把……分类；分开
5. schedule	时间表；计划表，日程安排表；目录，清单；报表
6. check out	结账后离开，退房
7. luggage	行李
8. in front of	在……的前面
9. bellman	行李员
10. pick up	捡起；拿；获得
11. confirm	确定；证实

 Part 3　Reading 快速阅读

Passage 1

Hotel Phoenix Singapore

　　While many hotels have their expansion stalled by the economic crisis, Hotel Phoenix Singapore is bucking the trend. It is adding more rooms, never minding that rates in Singapore have actually gone down. Travel Asia profiles how one of Singapore's older properties—Hotel Phoenix Singapore—is also one of its most progressive and forward thinking properties.

It has allotted $5.25 million in building 83 more hi-tech rooms and is doubling its function rooms to four.

Noel Hawkes who is the general manager explains, "We believe that a company that is not growing is dying and we see the economic downturn as an opportunity to expand and increase our facilities in preparation for the new millennium."

"We expect that the economy in Singapore and the region will be improved by the year 2000 and we will reap the benefits of our investment in the coming days."

The relocation of the medical center from the Specialist Shopping Center frees three floors in the hotel, of which two will be converted into super deluxe rooms and one will be converted into the executive floor.

Phoenix currently has 312 rooms and 2 existing executive floors. All super deluxe rooms will have an IDD telephone with voicemail in English, Mandarin and Japanese. A color TV with international channels such as CNN, NHK and in-house movie channels will also be provided. Ports will be provided to plug in laptops.

Guests without computers can stay in Phoenix's existing rooms which are provided with an NEC personal multimedia computer equipped with direct internet access, e-mail facilities, Microsoft Office, BigLobe Financial Website, Newspapers of the World, video-games, video and music CD players.

All the new rooms will also have the latest OSIM fully-automatic personal massage couches to help guests relieve stress, tension, aches and pains and improve blood circulation.

Guests will be given free entry to California Fitness Center, the largest gym in Singapore, which is two blocks away from the hotel.

Vocabulary

buck	抵制；反抗
circulation	循环；流通；发行量；通货
couch	睡椅，长沙发
currently	普遍地，通常，现在，当前
decline	下倾，下降，辞职，衰退；婉拒
downturn	衰落，降低
executive	实行的，执行的，行政的；高级享受的

expansion	扩充，膨胀
gym	体育馆；健身房
investment	投资
laptop	便携式计算机
Mandarin	国语，普通话
massage	按摩
millennium	太平盛世；千禧年
opportunity	时机，机会
phoenix	凤凰；完美之物
profile	简介，概况；侧面，外形；描出……的轮廓；给……画侧面像
progressive	进步的，前进的，现代的
property	财产，所有权，所有物
reap	获得；收割庄稼
region	地区，地域
relieve	减轻，救济，解除
relocation	迁址，换址
resolute	不屈不挠的，坚决的，果断的
stall	进退两难
trend	趋势，倾向

Phrases

blood circulation	血液循环
economic crisis	经济危机
massage couch	按摩椅，按摩床
go down	下沉，下降
provide with	提供……
reap the benefits	盈利
see... as	把……看作……
in preparation for	为……准备

| Singapore | 新加坡 |
| IDD telephone | 国际直拨电话 |

Passage 2

The Profile of Hilton

Ever since Conrad Hilton opened his first hotel in 1919, the Hilton organization has built a reputation for quality, value, integrity and strength. For more than 85 years, "Hilton" has been standing for excellence in the industry. Hilton Hotels Corporation includes more than 2,300 hotels in North America. Besides, it offers five-star luxury hotels in many places such as London, Tokyo, Hong Kong, Singapore and Bali. In addition to that, Hilton International has a global network, which provides its customers with 2,700 hotels in about 55 countries worldwide.

As one of the best brands in this field, it is not only well-known and well-respected, but also referred to as a market leader. Holding the belief, "Travel is more than just from A to B. Travel should inspire new ideas", it tries to deliver outstanding products, service and experiences to each customer.

In today's increasingly competitive hotel industry, the winners are those with the best brands that offer the most attractive marketing programs.

Hilton Hotels Corporation has been a leader in creating a diversity of programs. It is now able to offer guests the widest possible range of hotel experiences, including four-star city center hotels, convention properties, all-suite hotels, extended stay, mid-priced focused service, destination resorts, vacation ownership, airport hotels and

Unit 1   Reservation Service 预订服务

conference centers.

In 1999, the Corporation established a new family of brands: Doubletree, Embassy Suites Hotels, Hampton Inn, Hampton Inn & Suites and Homewood Suites by Hilton. In November 2000, Hilton Group and Hilton Hotels Corporation formed a joint venture company to expand their business on a worldwide basis. Owned equally by Hilton Group and Hilton Hotels Corporation, this joint venture will be headquartered in Brussels, Belgium.

Vocabulary

attractive	有吸引力的，漂亮的，诱人的
belief	相信，信念，信仰
brand	商标，品牌
competitive	竞争的

convention	习俗，会议，集会
destination	目的地，意图
diversity	不同，变化多端，不同点
establish	建立，确立
extend	延伸，伸展，扩大
headquarter	总部，总公司
industry	工业，产业
integrity	正直，诚实，完整
luxury	奢华的
offer	提供
ownership	所有权，所有制
reputation	名誉，声望
vacation	假期
well-known	著名的，众所周知的
worldwide	世界范围的

Phrases

marketing program	营销计划
joint venture	合资企业
be able to	有能力做……
refer to	涉及，提及
stand for	代表……的立场
in addition to	除……之外
not only... but also	不仅……而且

Terms

Conrad Hilton	康拉德·希尔顿
North America	北美洲
London	伦敦

Tokyo	东京
Bali	巴厘岛
Brussels	布鲁塞尔
Belgium	比利时

 Part 4 Writing 写作技巧

Reservation Letter
预 订 信

A reservation letter should be concise, specific and short. And it should include the type of room to be reserved, the exact date, the duration, the time of arrival and departure, and other personal references.

November 26, 2020

Dear Sales Manager,

We have a 16-people group visiting Brisbane, Australia from December 12th to 15th, 2020. We would like to have seven double rooms, two single rooms for three nights at your hotel. Please let us know at your earliest convenience if the rooms are available and send us the room tariff.

Yours,
Antony Yang
Tour Operator
Sunny Travel Service

Writing Practice

Write a reservation letter based on the following information.

Time: From September 30th to October 3rd, 2020

Destination: Gold Coast, Australia

Number of people: 19

Rooms needed: 6 doubles, 4 singles, 1 suite

Requirements: All non-smoking, ocean view

 Part 5　Vocabulary Expansion 词汇扩展

advance payment	预付款
bellboy	负责行李的男服务员
cashier	收银员
check-in	入住饭店
check-out	离开饭店
currency exchange	兑换货币
deposit	订金，保证金
front desk	前台
guest room	客房
guest source	客户资源
guest with reservation	预约的客人
information desk	信息台，咨询台
information tracing system	信息追踪系统
lobby	大厅
luggage deposit	行李寄存
large-scale hotel	大型酒店
leaving notice	离店通知单
lodge claim or complaint	提出索赔，提出意见
occupied room	有人入住的房间
periodic report	定期报告
receive a reservation	接受预订
switchboard	电话总机，服务台
wake-up service	唤醒服务
walk-in guest	没有预约的客人

Unit 2

Check-in Service 入住服务

> **Learning objectives 学习目标**
>
> After learning this unit, you should
> - learn how to ask and offer information about check-in at a hotel;
> - be familiar with the procedures of cheak-in;
> - organize the basic words and expressions used during check-in;
> - acquire some knowledge about check-in;
> - find ways to improve your writing skills in business reports.

 Part 1　Background knowledge 背景知识

An Introduction to Check-in at a Hotel 入住服务概述

At hotels or similar establishments, guests are usually required to check in, which involves confirming the guests' personal details and providing a signature. The establishment may require guests to provide a credit card guarantee to cover potential costs such as room service for the duration of the stay, and to enable an express check-out at the end of the stay. At the end of check-in, the reception staff will provide guests with a room key.

Hotels usually specify a check-in time after which they expect guests to check-in.

If a guest wants to occupy a hotel room before the hotel's check-in time, some hotels charge for an additional day or treat it as a previous day's stay. Most hotels, however, allow a grace time (typically 30~60 minutes) on request by a guest, without any additional charge, if a guest wishes to take the room before the check-in time. Some hotels also have a latest check-in time, often 6:00 p.m. -8:00 p.m., after which they may give a room to someone else if the room is not prepaid or the guest does not phone in to indicate a time of arrival. Some hotels have a deadline for checking-in because the reception may close at night. For the most cost-effective usage of hotel room occupancy, a guest should try to reach at about the hotel's check-in time and leave or hand over the hotel room at about the hotel's check-out time, but it may not be always practical because the guest's arrival and departure time of flights or car trips may not align with the hotel check-in and check-out time or for other reasons.

Unit 2　Check-in Service 入住服务

 Part 2　Speaking 对话训练

Dialogue 1

Checking In

(Mr. James is checking in at Heaven Hotel.　A: Receptionist; B: Mr. James)

A: Good afternoon. Welcome to Heaven Hotel. May I help you?

B: Yes, I'd like to check in, please.

A: Certainly, sir. May I have your name, please?

B: I'm James.

A: Do you have a reservation with us, Mr. James?

B: Yes, for two nights.

A: Just a moment, please. I'll check our reservation record. (After a while) Thank you for waiting, Mr. James. Your reservation is a twin room from December 6th to 8th for two nights. Is that all right?

B: Exactly.

A: Could you fill out the registration form, please?

B: Fine. (Fill in the form)

A: How would you like to make payment?

B: By Visa card.

A: May I take a print of the card, please?

B: Sure, here you are.

A: Thank you, Mr. James. Your room number is 1530, that's on the 15th floor. A bellman will show you the room. Please enjoy your stay.

1. registration　　　　　　　　　登记，注册
2. payment　　　　　　　　　　付款

Dialogue 2

Registering in a Hotel

(A: Receptionist; B: Guest)

A: Good afternoon. How may I help you?

B: Sure. I called to book a room at your hotel a week ago and my name is Tommy Gates. I'm from New York, the United States.

A: Just a minute, Mr. Gates. (After a while) Ah, yes. Tommy Gates from New York. A single room from today till Thursday, July 7th.

B: Yes.

A: Please fill in the form, sir.

B: There you go. Is that okay?

A: It's perfect. Here is your room card, sir. Your room number is 908. It's on the 9th floor.

B: How can I get to the 9th floor?

A: Don't worry. A bellboy will come and take you to your room.

B: Thank you very much.

A: You're welcome and enjoy your stay.

B: I will.

1. room card   房卡
2. perfect   非常好

 Part 3   Reading 快速阅读

Understanding Customer Behavior—
Patchwork Quilt Country Inn

In our fast-paced society, many people use their weekends and vacations to escape from the stresses and strains of everyday life. They have a need to relax—to have a change of pace in their lifestyles. Bed & breakfast and farm vacation operations have grown in popularity because of this need and behavioral characteristic. Their increased use is also a result of the high value offered for the same amount of money when compared to other lodging alternatives.

The Patchwork Quilt Country Inn, located in Northern Indiana near Middlebury, is an excellent example of a small bed & breakfast operation. It has enjoyed great success by capitalizing on some basic human needs and motivations. It began in 1962 on the Lovejoy farm when the Lovejoys started taking people in for vacations at their 260-acre dairy farm. Mrs. Lovejoy's recipes and cooking proved so popular that the family decided to open a small restaurant. After the restaurant became successful, a three-room bed & breakfast operation was started in the converted farmhouse. The Inn's facilities now include 15 guest rooms, each with a private bathroom and a sitting room. The dining areas have a total of 80 seats. Bed & breakfast guests are served a full breakfast. At lunch and dinner, the dining rooms are open to the public. The Inn is renowned for the healthy, fresh ingredients in its menu items, and for the fact that all cooking and baking is done "from scratch" on the premises. Several recipes are unique, including the Buttermilk Pecan Chicken and some pies. The Inn has a strict no-smoking policy and does not serve or allow any alcoholic beverages.

Why use the name Patchwork Quilt Country Inn? First, the operation is located in the heart of "Northern Indiana's Amish Country", an area of 150 square miles around Goshen, the second largest Amish settlement in the United States. Quilting, of course, is a craft closely associated with the Amish people of North America. Additionally, the theme is carried through in the Inn's decor and advertising materials. Beds are covered with beautiful patchwork quilts, and quilts also adorn dining room walls and other parts of the Inn. Even the Inn's logo incorporates the patchwork quilt theme. Quilts and other local crafts can be purchased at the Inn.

The main advertising slogan is "Prepare to Be Pampered" and the invitation to "Enjoy a Taste of the Country" is added in the Inn's main brochure. These statements suggest motives to potential guests involving a visit to the Inn. Seeing the brochure or other advertising, readers may become aware of their need to "get away from it all", to relax and escape into a simpler life in the country. The Inn's objectives are marketed to potential customers, and these customers' needs become wants through having been made aware of the service. Several of these potential customers will be so highly motivated by the Inn's marketing and services, along with the recognition of their need deficiencies, that they will make reservations.

The Patchwork Quilt Country Inn has received national recognition through various feature articles and listings in popular bed & breakfast/country inn guidebooks such as *Country Inns* and *BackRoads*. While most of the Inn's advertisings are targeted in the surrounding Midwest region, especially in Michigan and Indians, guests come from all over the country. Ads are placed in magazines such as *Great Lakes Travel*, *Country Homes*, and *Midwest Living*, and in newspapers in Kalamazoo, Grand Rapids, and Wayne as well as local newspapers. The current innkeepers, Ray and Rosetta Miller, are also experimenting with radio advertising. Although the Inn does not use television advertising, it receives many requests from TV stations to do feature stories. Two types of guests tend to predominate: older and retired persons, and younger couples on weekend getaways. A significant amount of business comes through word-of-mouth.

In the early 1980s, the Inn began to offer Amish Backroad Tours. These are 3 hours' guided tours in a van or car, involving sightseeing and visits to several Amish homes and businesses. Guests get a first-hand look at Amish craft making and other facets of Amish way of life. This programming feature fits well with the Inn's overall appeal to travelers' motivations, allowing them to take a step back to an even simpler lifestyle.

Bed & breakfast is available year round at the Inn. The restaurant is closed in

January. Dinner is served on Friday in March and April, and Tuesday through Saturday from April to December. Lunch is served from May to December on Tuesday through Saturday. Lunches and dinners are not served on Sundays, Mondays, or public holidays. The B&B rates are $70 ~ $110 (per day, per room on a double occupancy basis). Sales tax is added, and a 15 percent gratuity is also put on meals.

It is easy to see how the simple, healthy lifestyle offered by the Patchwork Quilt Country Inn and other similar bed and breakfast operations is a perfect antidote for the city dwellers whose lives move at a rapid pace. While they must be resigned to spending most of their lives in traffic jams and with hectic work schedules, it is refreshing to return for a day or two to a more relaxed environment. The Patchwork Quilt Country Inn is an excellent example of a business that makes people aware of their needs, and then satisfies those needs with caring, quality service, and beautiful facilities.

Vocabulary

adorn	装饰；使生色
alternative	供选择的；选择性的；二中择一
alcoholic	酒精的，含酒精的；酒鬼，酗酒者
antidote	［药］解毒剂；解药；矫正方法
behavioral	行为的
brochure	手册，小册子
characteristic	典型的；特有的；特征；特色
capitalize	利用；积累资本；估计……的价值
convert	转变，变换；皈依
craft	工艺；手艺；太空船；精巧地制作
decor	装饰，装潢；装饰品；奖章
deficiency	缺陷，缺点；缺乏；不足的数额
experiment	尝试；进行实验；实验，试验
facet	面；方面；小平面
feature	特征；容貌；起重要作用；以……为特色
ingredient	原料；要素；组成部分；构成组成部分的

incorporate	包含，吸收；体现；把……合并
lifestyle	生活方式
lodging	寄宿；出租的房间、住房
motivation	动机；积极性；推动
patchwork	拼缝物，拼缀物；混杂物
popularity	普及，流行；名气；受大众欢迎
predominate	支配，主宰；在……中占优势
quilt	被子；棉被；东拼西凑地编
recipe	食谱；处方
renowned	著名的；有声望的；使有声誉
recognition	识别；承认，认出；重视；赞誉；公认
resign	辞职；放弃；委托；使听从
strain	张力；拉紧；负担
scratch	擦伤；抓痕；乱写；打草稿用的
slogan	标语；呐喊声
target	目标；靶子；把……作为目标；瞄准
word-of-mouth	口碑

Phrases

a result of	……的结果
a total of	全部的
appeal to	对……上诉；引起兴趣
be located in	位于……
become aware of	对……有知觉，开始意识到
potential customer	潜在顾客
traffic jam	交通堵塞

Terms

Midwest region	美国中西部

Michigan   美国密歇根州

Northern Indiana 印第安纳州北部

 Part 4　Writing 写作技巧

Business Report
商务报告

Types of business report: informal and formal

Informal business report

(1) is either in a letter or a memorandum format;

(2) is short and concise;

(3) includes four parts: introduction, body, conclusion and suggestion;

(4) is widely used in tourism business.

Formal business report

(1) is very formal and objective;

(2) can run as long as hundreds of pages;

(3) is used for grand project only.

Accident Report

To: Department Officer

From: Chen Zhong, National Guide, Beijing GITS

Date: May 15, 2020

Subject: Traffic Accident Report

Introduction

Group HP-2020-023 arrived in our city on May 12, 2020 and finished a whole day sightseeing on May 13, 2020 according to the itinerary. Unfortunately, a traffic accident happened late in the afternoon on the way back to the hotel. This is a written report of the accident for your information.

Accident description

On the way back from the museum to the hotel at about 16:00 on May 13, 10 km away from the city, a truck suddenly swerved towards our tour bus when it tried to dodge another coming truck, our driver responded with a sudden brake and fortunately avoided a clash. As a consequence of the sudden stop, two members of the group who did not fasten their seatbelts were thrown off their seats. One got his upper lip hurt and the other got her nose hurt. They were sent to the nearest hospital immediately with the help of 120 ambulance (First Aid Service) accompanied by the tour leader and me. They went through all the necessary checking and treatment procedures at the hospital. After necessary examinations have been done, the hospital was confident to release them and provided the medical check reports.

We have also received the report from the local police. The report stated clearly that it was the other party's full responsibility. The two injured members continued the rest of their trip. As compensation, the general manager of the local travel agency sent flowers to each person to their hotel rooms and treated them with a special dinner that night. All the members of the group were very grateful to our driver for his adequate response to the emergency and were satisfied with our timely handling of the matter.

We feel sorry for what had happened and we will see to it that more safety measures are strengthened in the future.

+-+

Writing Practice

One of your group members lost his passport. Write a report in the name of a local guide to the tour organizer in London to inform how the case was handled.

Part 5　Vocabulary Expansion 词汇扩展

cafe	咖啡厅
coupon	优待券
cash a check	兑现支票
corridor	走廊
exchange memo	外汇兑换水单

lounge	休闲室，酒廊
switch	开关
today's exchange rate	今天的兑换率
the parking lot	停车场
thermostat	温控器，恒温器

Unit 3

Housekeeping Service 客房服务

> **Learning objectives** 学习目标
>
> After learning this unit, you should
> - read, comprehend and translate into Chinese the dialogues about housekeeping;
> - acquire the knowledge about how to give information about housekeeping;
> - organize the basic words and expressions about housekeeping service and use them to make sentences;
> - learn some cultural knowledge about housekeeping service;
> - practice the dialogues and talk about housekeeping;
> - find ways to improve your writing skills in resumes on applying for jobs.

 Part 1　Background knowledge 背景知识

1. Types of Hotel Rooms 客房类型

(1) single room　　　　　　单人房

　　double room　　　　　　双人房

　　standard room　　　　　标准房

　　triple room　　　　　　三人房

(2) economy room 经济房
standard room 标准房
superior room 高级房
deluxe room 豪华房
standard suite 标准套房
presidential suite 总统套房

(3) run of the house 不限房型
non-smoking room 无烟房
handicapped room 残疾人客房
room with kitchen 带厨房客房
adjoining room 相邻房
(4) studio room 工作室型客房（设沙发床或躺椅）
multi-functional room 多功能客房
combined-type room 组合客房

2. Types of Restaurants 饭店种类

inn 旅馆
lodge 小旅馆
tavern 酒店，客栈
caravansary 马车店，大旅馆
hostel 旅社，招待所（尤指青年旅社）

hotel 饭店，酒店

motel（=motor hotel）	汽车饭店（旅馆）
budget hotel	经济型旅馆
economy hotel（one-star hotel）	一星级酒店
some comfort hotel（two-star hotel）	二星级酒店
average hotel（three-star hotel）	三星级酒店
high comfort hotel（four-star hotel）	四星级酒店
deluxe hotel（five-star hotel）	五星级酒店

Unit 3   Housekeeping Service 客房服务

Part 2   Speaking 对话训练

Dialogue 1

Happy Birthday

(H: Housekeeper; G: Guest)

H: May I come in, Mr. Paul?

G: Come in, please.

H: I'm here to say "Happy Birthday" to you.

G: Thank you. How do you know it is my birthday today?

H: We learned from the registration record. Please accept this birthday card and these flowers from us attendants.

G: I really appreciate your congratulations. It is very considerate of you.

H: My pleasure!

Dialogue 2

Changing a Room

(H: Housekeeper; G: Guest)

H: Is this Room 3201?

G: Yes, it is.

H: You said the toilet doesn't work and we sent a repairman to fix it, but it's hard to fix it at once. I'm afraid you have to change a room.

G: Change a room? How long does it need?

H: At least one day.

G: OK. Where shall I move to?

H: Room 3421. The bellman will help you soon. I'm sorry for the inconvenience.

G: Never mind.

Dialogue 3

Seeing Off Guests

(H: Housekeeper; G: Guest)

G: Excuse me, may I have the bill? I'm leaving in an hour. I'm going to pay my account right now.

H: Yes, madam. Here you are. That's the total amount of payment at the bottom there.

G: Thank you. I don't want to come back to the room after I settle my bill at the cashier's counter. May I take my baggage downstairs now?

H: Of course. Have you got your baggage ready?

G: Yes, I have packed everything up.

H: Shall I have the bellman help you with your stuff?

G: No, thank you. I can handle that by myself. I have only two bags. They're not too heavy.

H: Fine. Would you mind my checking the room?

G: Of course not. Let's go, shall we?

H: Yes, let's go. Is everything to your satisfaction during your stay here?

G: Yes, I'm quite satisfied. I had a good time at your hotel.

H: After you, madam.

G: Now please do your duty.

H: Thank you for your cooperation. The desk lamp is there. The vacuum-flask is not broken. Here are teacups and the saucer. The TV set is all right. Very good. You may go now. May I have the key back?

G: Yes, here it is.

H: Thank you. Let me carry one of the bags to the lift for you.

G: Many thanks. Let's be off now.

H: Here comes the lift. I wish you a pleasant journey. Goodbye.

Notes

1. registration record   登记本
2. attendant   服务员
3. considerate   体贴的，周到的
4. appreciate one's congratulations   感激某人的祝贺

5. repairman 修理工
6. pack up 打包，收拾
7. Would you mind doing sth.? 您介意做某事吗？
8. do one's duty 履行责任
9. cooperation 合作
10. desk lamp 台灯
11. vacuum-flask 热水瓶
12. saucer 茶托

 Part 3　Reading 快速阅读

Passage 1

Tips on Service

Hotel workers depend on tips to augment their usually small salaries. Rather than being annoyed at having to tip the doorman who greets you, consider it as part of the cost of travel and be prepared with the dollar bills you will need to hand out before you even get to your room.

Doorman

Depending on the amount of luggage, tip $1 to $2 to the doorman who takes your bags and turns them over to a bellman. If you are visiting and have no luggage, you naturally do not tip him for simply opening the door for you. Tip him again when you leave with your luggage as he takes it from the bellman and assists you in loading it in your car or taxi. When the doorman obtains a taxi for you, tip him $1 to $3 (or higher amount if he must stand in the rain for a period of time to get it).

Bellman

Tip more than $1 a bag but less than $2 to the bellman who carries or delivers your luggage to your room. When the bellman does something special for you, such as make a purchase or bring something you have requested to your room, but not room service deliveries, he or she should be tipped $2 to $3 for every service at the time it is provided.

Maid

For stays of one night or more, the maid should be tipped $2 per night per person in a large hotel; $1 per night per person in a less expensive hotel. Give the maid her tip in person, if she can be found. If not, put it in a sealed envelope marked "chambermaid".

Valet

Valet services are added to your bill, so there is no need to tip for pressing or cleaning when items are left in your room. If you are in your room when your cleaning and pressing is delivered, however, tip ＄1 for the delivery for one or two items, tip more when several items are being delivered.

Dining room staff

Tips for dining room staff are exactly the same as they are in any other restaurants—15 to 18 percent except in the most elegant dining rooms where tips are 18 to 20 percent. If you are staying in an American-plan hotel where your meals are included in your total bill, tips are as usual, and an additional tip should be given to the maitre who has taken care of you during your stay. This tip ranges anywhere from ＄10 to ＄15 for a weekend for a family or group of four people from ＄20 to ＄30 for a longer stay or a larger group.

Vocabulary

annoy	使……恼火
assist	协助，帮助
chambermaid	清理房间的服务员
deliver	投递，送
doorman	门卫
elegant	优雅的
purchase	购买
press	熨烫
valet	清洗、熨烫衣服的服务员

Phrases

additional tip	额外的小费
dining room staff	餐厅服务员
depend on	依赖，取决于
take care of	照看，照顾

Passage 2

Etiquette of British Bars

Amazingly for the British, who love queues, there is no formal line-up when ordering drinks at a British bar—the bar staff are skilled at knowing whose turn it is. You are permitted to try to attract attention, but there are rules about how to do this. Do not call out, tap coins on the counter, snap your finger or wave like a drowning swimmer. Do not scowl or sigh or roll your eyes. And whatever you do, do not ring the bell hanging behind the counter this is used by the landlord to signal closing time. The key thing is to catch the bar worker's eyes. You could also hold an empty glass or some money, but do not wave them about. Do adopt an expectant, hopeful, even slightly anxious facial expression. If you look too contented and complacent, the bar staff may assume you are already being served.

Always say "please" and try to remember some of the British bar staff's pet hates. They do not like people to keep others waiting while they make up their minds. They do not like people to keep standing idly against the bar when there are a lot of customers waiting for service. And they do not like people who wait until the end of the order before asking for such drinks as Guinness stout which take considerably longer to pour than other drinks.

One Dutch tourist who spent 6 months on visiting 800 of Britain's 61,000 pubs and interviewing 50 publicans and bar workers and more than 1,000 customers said, "I cannot understand how the British ever manage to buy themselves a drink." But they do, and if you follow these tips you should be able to do so, too.

Speaking of tips, you should never offer the bar staff a cash gratuity. The correct behavior is to offer them a drink. Pubs pride themselves on their egalitarian atmosphere.

A tip in cash would be a reminder of their service role, whereas the offer of a drink is a friendly gesture.

Vocabulary

amazingly	令人惊讶地
atmosphere	大气,空气,气氛
complacent	自满的,得意的
contented	满足的,心安的
considerably	相当地
egalitarian	平等主义的,平等主义
gratuity	赠物,赏钱
Guinness	吉尼斯黑啤酒
interview	接见,会见
permit	通行证,许可证,执照
publican	收税员,酒馆老板
scowl	愁容,怒容
snap	捻(手指)发噼啪声
stout	结实的,勇敢坚定的;烈性黑啤酒

Part 4 Writing 写作技巧

Resume
简 历

A resume is a list of a person's qualifications for a job and is enclosed with a letter of application. It is made up of five categories of information.

1. Personal details including name, mailing address, telephone number, etc. ;
2. Educational background;
3. Work experiences;
4. Basic skills such as language level, computer skills and other relevant skills;
5. Location of credentials, which include letters of recommendation.

Resume

Liu Xiao

Huang Cheng University, China 100031

Tel: 0086-10-8675230

E-mail: Liux@hcu.com

Education

2017—2021 BA degree from Management Department

　　　　　Huang Cheng University

　　　　　Major: Hotel Management

Honors

2019 University Second Class Scholarship

Activities

2020 vice president of University Student Union

Work experiences

2020—2021 part-time teacher at the training center of Dream Inn Beijing, assistant training manager of the HRM Department

2019—2020 English tutor for middle school students

Basic skills

English：CET-6（Score：550）

Computer：Microsoft Office

Special Interests：traveling，music

References：available upon request

-+-

Writing Practice

Refer to the writing sample, and practice writing a resume based on your own information.

Part 5　Vocabulary Expansion 词汇扩展

assistant manager	副经理
automatic sliding door	自动滑动门
briefcase	公文包
baggage receipt	行李收据
cigarette deposit	香烟托盘
duty manager	值班经理
executive housekeeper	行政管家
elevator operator	电梯工
front office	前厅
front office clerk	前台收银员
foreign exchange clerk	外币兑换员
guest relations officer	宾客关系主任
hair dryer	吹风机
hotel bill	旅馆账单
information supervisor	信息主管
key rack	钥匙存放架
letter rack	信件存放架
manager of room division	客房部经理

name tag	标有姓名的标签
register	旅馆登记簿，登记
reception supervisor	接待部主管
registration form	登记卡
rate sheet	房价表
security guard	保安员
shower head	淋浴喷头
storage room	行李仓；库房
suit bag	衣服袋
trolley	手推车
television remote control	电视遥控器
traveling bag	旅行袋
ventilator	换气扇
valuables	贵重品
wall lamp	壁灯

Unit 4

Food & Beverage Service 餐饮服务

Learning objectives 学习目标

After learning this unit, you should

- read, comprehend and translate the passages and dialogues about food and beverage into Chinese;
- acquire the knowledge about how to give information about food and beverage;
- organize the basic words and expressions about food and beverage and use them to make sentences;
- learn some cultural knowledge about food and beverage;
- practice the dialogues and talk about food and beverage;
- find ways to improve your writing skills in recruitment advertisement.

 Part 1　Background knowledge 背景知识

Drinking

Drinking habits vary widely among Americans as they do among people from other lands. Some families never serve any alcoholic drinks, others have them before dinner, during dinner, and perhaps after dinner. You are more likely to be offered a cocktail before dinner than with the meal. If you are not accustomed to American cocktails, be careful, they are often quite strong. In some homes, cocktails may be served for an hour or longer before dinner. If you do not wish to have another cocktail, simply say "No, thanks".

Wine is becoming increasingly popular with Americans but is still not common in the old world, or widely accepted as beer does. Do not be surprised if you are offered milk, coffee, tea (iced or hot, depending on the season) or even Coca-Cola with a meal. Water is usually served in restaurants without being ordered, although you may certainly order anything else you prefer to drink.

Eating out—Who Pays?

If you've made an agreement to go out to eat with someone, you should be clear who's paying. If the other person suggests you have lunch with him or her, you might simply say something like this, "I'm afraid it'll have to be someplace inexpensive as I have very little money." The other person may say, "OK, I'll meet you at McDonald." This means that you've agreed that each person pays for his own meal. You can also say "go Dutch." If the person says, "Oh, no, I want to take you to lunch in a little restaurant I like very much." It means that the person intends to pay the bill for both of you. If a person invites you to his or her home for a meal, it's understood that that person is paying; if you invite someone to your home, it's understood that you are buying the food. If you want to invite someone out for lunch, you must also make yourself clear by saying, perhaps, "I'd like to take you to lunch tomorrow at the Hostess Inn Coffee Shop," (meaning you plan to buy the food), or "Let's have lunch together tomorrow at Burger King. It's on me." American women used to expect men to pay for all meals, but today most women will pay for themselves. However, you should always make your position clear. Being clear is the polite thing to do; it is lack of clarity that causes loss of face in this situation.

Part 2 Speaking 对话训练

Dialogue 1

At the Chinese Restaurant

(Scene: The waiter is explaining something to Johnson. J: Johnson; W: Waiter)

J: Excuse me, I'd like to try some Chinese food. Can you tell me where I should go?

W: We serve Chinese food here. But I'm not sure which style you prefer.

J: I have no idea about Chinese food.

W: It's divided into four big cuisines, or say four styles. They are Cantonese cuisine, Beijing cuisine, Sichuan food and Shanghai food.

J: Is there any difference between Cantonese food and Beijing food?

W: Yes, Cantonese food is lighter while Beijing food is heavy and salty. The famous specialties of these two are aromatic suckling piggy and Beijing roast duck.

J: How about Sichuan food?

W: Most Sichuan dishes are spicy and hot. And they taste different.

J: Oh, really, I like spicy food. So what's your recommendation for me?

W: I think Mapo beancurd and shredded meat in chilli sauce are quite special. We have a Sichuan food dining room. May I suggest you go there? It's on the second floor.

J: Thank you.

W: My pleasure.

Notes

1. cuisine   烹饪，烹饪法
2. light   清淡的，易消化的
3. heavy   难消化的
4. spicy   香的；加香料的；香辣的
5. Cantonese   广东的
6. specialty   特制的，特产
7. aromatic suckling piggy   烤乳猪
8. Beijing roast duck   北京烤鸭
9. hot   刺激的，辣的
10. chilli   （干）辣椒

Dialogue 2

Having Chinese Food

(A: Waiter; B: Mr. Frank)

A: Mr. Frank, what would you like to have tonight, Western food or Chinese food?

B: When I was in America, my friend, Mr. Dull recommended me to have Chinese food, and I appreciate it very much indeed. What kind of cuisine do you have in your dining room?

A: We have Cantonese food, Sichuan food and Shanghai food. Which one do you like best?

B: I don't like anything greasy. I think I'd like to have Cantonese food.

A: OK. How about sauté prawn section, sauté lobster slices with mushroom?

B: All right. I'll take them both.

A: Mr. Frank, do you like to use chopsticks? If you don't, I'll get you fork and knife.

B: Fork and knife, please.

A: OK, and would you like some soup?

B: Yes, I don't know what soup you have.

A: We have sliced chicken soup, dried mushroom clear soup and so on.

B: Good. I prefer dried mushroom clear soup.

A: According to the specifications of Chinese food, we serve dishes first and then soup. If you like we'll bring you some soup first.

B: I'm used to having soup first.

A: All right, I'll get it for you.

Notes

1. greasy	油腻的
2. sauté	嫩煎的，用少量油快炸的
3. lobster	龙虾
4. mushroom	蘑菇
5. specification	规格，说明书

Dialogue 3

At the Western Restaurant

(Scene: Wang Hong, the tour guide recommends a western restaurant to Mr. and Mrs. Brown. The couple is having their dinner in the restaurant. G: Tour Guide; W: Waiter; T: Tourist)

T2: Darling, these days we have tasted different Chinese dishes of different styles. I want to have western food for a change today.

T1: Oh, Miss Wang, do you know any good western food restaurants around here?

G: Yes, there is a Red Rose Restaurant nearby, which serves western food. I'd like to make a reservation for you if you want.

T1: Thank you. Please make a reservation at 7:00 tonight.

G: All right.

(At the Restaurant)

W: Good evening!

T1: Good evening! I'm Mr. Brown. We have a reservation.

W: This way, please. Your table is near the window.

T2: Thank you.

W: Here is the menu.

T1: Thank you.

G: May I take your order?

T1: We haven't decided yet. Could you give us a little more time?

W: Yes, take your time, please.

T1: Can we get something to drink? I want a bottle of beer. My wife wants a cup of coffee.

W: Fine.

T1: Could you tell us your specials today?

W: The special today is steak.

T1: I'll take this steak for dinner. My wife will have the same.

W: How would you like your steak?

T1: I'd like it medium-rare.

T2: I'd like it well-done.

W: What would you like to go with your steak?

T2: Peas and carrots.

T1: The same for me, please.

W：What would you like for dessert?

T1：Ice cream, please.

T2：No, thanks.

T1：Could I have the check, please?

W：Here's the check.

T1：Can I pay for the bill by credit card?

W：Yes, of course. Here's your receipt.

Notes

1. Chinese dishes   中国菜
2. western food   西餐
3. for a change   变换一下（口味）
4. around here   附近
5. Red Rose Restaurant   红玫瑰餐厅
6. menu   菜单
7. order   点菜
8. a bottle of beer   一瓶啤酒
9. a cup of coffee   一杯咖啡
10. steak dinner   牛排餐
11. medium-rare   嫩的（三至四分熟）
12. well-done   全熟的
13. peas and carrots   豌豆和胡萝卜
14. dessert   甜点
15. check   账单
16. receipt   收据

Part 3 Reading 快速阅读

Passage 1

American Food Habits

Generally speaking, American food is rather bland and not spicy. Salads are popular and are served all the year round. Many American people are trying to keep down their weight and so they are "calorie-conscious". This is evident in menus offering "low calorie" or "weight watchers" meals. In markets one can find "No CAL" drinks (meaning without calories) such as ginger ale or cola. "Diet" foods without sugar or salt are also available in food stores.

Waiters in American restaurants tend to assume that everyone drinks coffee. If a waiter suddenly asks "Now or later?" what he means is "Do you want coffee with your meal now or later?" Many Americans drink coffee with meal. When dining out in the US we can ask for tea, milk, coke, beer, and so on, if we prefer these to coffee. American restaurants cannot serve beer, wine, or liquor unless they are licensed to do so.

The main course in American meals is usually meat, fowl or fish, but rarely is more than one of these served in the same meal (except that seafood can be used as an appetizer).

Unit 4 Food & Beverage Service 餐饮服务

Vocabulary

assume	以为；假定
bland	清淡的
calorie	卡路里
conscious	意识到的
fowl	家禽

Phrases

ginger ale	姜汽水
keep down	控制

Passage 2

British Eating Habits

The British are traditionally conservative about their food and eating habits. But much of the food eaten in Britain now is not, in fact, traditional. The traditional cooked breakfast, for example, has been disappearing from homes and hotels in Britain. More and more people are interested in buying "convenience foods". Traditional foods are manufactured and processed and ready to cook or eat. Fresh fruit is a natural convenience food, available all the year round. With the changes in society, meals are becoming less

51

formal now. Snacks have become popular, and they can be eaten anywhere at any time.

An even more convenient way to eat is to buy food from a "take-away" (can be eaten either at home or in the take-away shop). This is quicker than cooking a meal and cheaper than eating in a restaurant. The most common take-away foods in Britain are fish and chips, hamburgers, and Chinese food.

More recently, there has occurred a new change in the diet. As processed foods made in factories are believed to contain additives and be affected by chemical fertilizers, some people have turned their interest to natural foods. They would prefer a diet of nuts, honey, dried fruits, and naturally grown cereals and vegetables. Special "Health Food Stores", and even supermarkets now sell such natural health foods.

additive　　　　　　　　　　　　添加剂

occur	发生
conservative	保守的
contain	包括
cereal	谷物，麦片
fertilizer	肥料
manufacture	生产，加工
nut	坚果
snack	快餐；小吃
take-away	外卖餐馆
supermarket	超级市场

Part 4　Writing 写作技巧

Help-wanted Advertisements
招聘广告

Like other kinds of advertisements, help-wanted advertisements are media-oriented. In order to be economical, help-wanted advertisements in newspapers are usually short. No matter in newspapers or online, help-wanted advertisements generally include the following information.

Contact Information

(1) Business name

(2) Business address

(3) Business phone

(4) Business e-mail address

Or

(5) Contact person's name

(6) Contact person's phone

(7) Contact person's e-mail address

(8) Contact person's mailing address

Job Information

(1) Position title

(2) Location

(3) Business name

(4) Job description

(5) Qualifications

(6) Benefits

(7) Days & hours of employment

(8) Salary range

In addition, please pay attention to writing with characteristics and styles. Help-wanted advertisements should

(1) Create Some Novel Headings

Examples:

Hero Meets Hero

It Is You Who Make Everything Possible

(2) Utilize Various Kinds of Phrases

Examples:

Good communication skills

Ability to work in a team under pressure

(3) Use Imperative Sentences Frequently

Examples:

Please apply in your own handwriting with full English resume and send photos to...

Please highlight the position you apply for at the bottom of the envelope.

Please call 0810-5808123-3629 for an interview.

(4) Make Use of Abbreviations

Examples:

Dept. = department	部门
CV = curriculum vitae	个人简历
JV = joint venture	合资
G. M. = general manager	总经理

Ad = advertisement　　　　　　　广告

Add = address　　　　　　　　 地址

ID = identification　　　　　　 身份证

One Native English Speaking Teacher Required

School：×××Teachers College

Position：oral English teacher

Expected Date：currently available

Location：Cangzhou, Hebei Province.

Requirements

1. native English speaker

2. teaching experience and BA degree

3. female teacher preferred

Job description

1. oral English courses

2. 16 hours a week

3. about 30 college students from 18 to 24 years old in each class

4. at least one year contract or longer

Remuneration Package

1. monthly salary：negotiable

2. one round trip airfare for one year duration

3. one private furnished apartment and utilities provided

4. public holidays and one-month annual vacation with pay

Contact

Name：Zhang Hua

Add：English Department, XXX Teachers College, Cangzhou, Hebei, China, 061001

Tel：0311-83998833

E-mail：ZhangH@ eng. com

Posting Date：October 23, 2020

Writing Practice

Organize the following information into a help-wanted advertisement.

Business Address：5026 NBroadway or 2815 W Montrose

Fax No.：773-463-7435

E-mail Address：contact@ neonexpressl. com

Position Title：secretary/administrative assistant

Application Dates and Hours：Monday—Friday, 9：00 a. m. —4：00 p. m.

Qualifications：good communication, bilingual, basic computer skills (Microsoft Word and Excel)

Salary Range：＄8～＄10/hour

Part 5 Vocabulary Expansion 词汇扩展

appetizer	开胃菜
alcoholic beverage	含酒精饮料
boiled	煮的
braised pork	扣肉
blanched prawn	白灼海虾
braised carp in brown sauce	红烧鲤鱼
buttered toast	涂了黄油的烤面包
clear soup of three delicious ingredients	三鲜汤
corn-and-hot soup	杂菜汤
chicken with cashew nuts	腰果鸡丁
continental breakfast	欧洲大陆式早餐
deep-fried	油炸的
fried peanut	油炸花生米
fish and seafood	鱼与海鲜
fried egg	煎蛋
kidney bean	四季豆
medium	五分熟

medium well	七分熟
mineral water	矿泉水
main course	主菜
pickled Chinese onion	腌大葱
pickled cucumber	腌黄瓜
pork braised in brown sauce	红烧肉
preserved egg	皮蛋
rare	一分熟
roast mutton	烤羊肉
rice noodles	粉条，米粉
steamed	蒸的
salad	沙拉，凉拌菜
sandwich	三明治
salted vegetable	咸菜
smoked duck	熏鸭
sweet dumpling	汤圆
steamed meat dumpling	小笼包
soft drink	软饮料，不含酒精的饮料
walnut seeds with mushrooms	桃仁冬菇

Unit 5

Banquet Service 宴会服务

> **Learning objectives 学习目标**
>
> After learning this unit, you should
> - acquire the knowledge about the types of banquet service;
> - organize the basic words and expressions about banquet service;
> - learn some cultural knowledge about banquet service;
> - find ways to improve your writing skills in letters of complaints;
> - be familiar with some Chinese & Western dishes.

 Part 1　Background knowledge 背景知识

Types of Banquet Service 宴会服务类型

It's important to decide on the types of service used at a banquet. Each service costs differently from one another.

1. American service (also known as plate service): It is the most common form of banquet service. The food is at the kitchen and waiters send the plates to the table from the left to the guest. At the end of course, the plates are picked up from the right.

2. Russian service (aslo known as platter service): Food is served from platters and waiters work as teams. They place food items on the diners' plates.

3. French service: It requires much space between tables for waiters to move around. With this service, a gueridon (餐厅里上菜用的小桌子) is set at the table side and food is prepared on the gueridon.

4. Preset service: It is a faster service that is often used for lunches. The first course of soup, salad or appetizer is set on the table before the guest arrives.

5. Buffet service: It is a display of food items on tables, so that attendees can select food for their own. This service may combine with other styles. For example, a banquet may begin with a buffet and then a sit-down dinner served by plate style; or the first and dessert courses are served by waiters and the main dishes by the buffet style.

 Part 2　Speaking 对话训练

Dialogue 1

Serving the Western Style Banquet

(Scene: The waiting staff is serving a western style banquet.)

Staff: You're at Table 18. Here we are. Take your seat, please.

Customer: I'm nearly late. Listen, our host is making the speech.

Staff: Yes. Let me fill your glass with brandy. The host is raising his glass for a toast.

Host: Ladies and gentlemen, may I propose a toast to the health of you all? Cheers!

Customer: Hey, this dish looks like a squirrel. What on earth is it?

Staff: This is the squirrel-shaped mandarin fish.

Customer: Wonderful, isn't it?

Staff: Yes. Please stay a little bit far away from the plate. When broth is poured, it might splash.

Customer: How does it taste?

Staff: It tastes crispy, with sour and sweet flavors. Here is one portion for you. Would you try the flavors yourself?

Customer: Hum, well, it is so soft inside.

Staff: May I take this plate away?

Customer: OK. What desserts do we have tonight?

Staff: Mango pudding and homemade cheese cake.

Customer: When will fruits come?

Staff: Just a minute, please. Here is your fruit knife. Do be careful.

Host: Ladies and gentlemen, thank you for your coming this evening.

Staff: Do you enjoy your meal this evening?

Customer: Yes, everything is fine.

Staff: I'm glad to hear it. This is your coat, sir. Good night.

Notes

1. host   主人，主持人
2. brandy   白兰地
3. broth   肉汤
4. splash   溅
5. crispy   脆的
6. flavor   味道
7. portion   （一）份
8. raise one's glass for a toast   举杯祝酒
9. homemade cheese cake   自制奶酪蛋糕

Dialogue 2

Serving the Buffet Dinner

Scene: At the Pacific Restaurant, a new buffet has been opened to attract customers. Now a server (S) is assisting a customer (C).

S: What can I do for you, sir?

C: Yes, Could you tell me what is included in the price?

S: Well. Our "All You Can Eat" salad bar allows you to return and get as much food as you like. New plates are provided at the far end of the bar.

C: How about drinks?

S: Only with 6 yuan extra can you get a cup of juice with free refill. May I also recommend this month's "Happy Hour" meal for drinks between 5:00 p.m. and 7:00 p.m.?

C: OK, we'll have a try. Where is the sauce?

S: You can find sauces, dressings and condiments near the fruit section of the salad bar.

C: This dish doesn't have an English name. Could you describe it for me please?

S: All right. This dish is the popular turkey sausages with turnip.

C: Sounds OK to me. Where could I find a serving spoon?

S: Here you are. Is this big enough?

C: Sure. Thanks.

S: My pleasure. Anything else I can do for you?

C: We're so hungry. We'll start eating. Thanks.

S: Sure. Let me know if I could be of further help. Please enjoy your buffet.

Notes

1. free refill   免费续杯
2. sauce   调味酱，沙司
3. dressing   调料
4. condiment   辛辣调味品
5. sausage   香肠
6. turnip   萝卜，芜菁
7. "All You Can Eat"   "请君选用"
8. salad bar   沙拉吧台

Part 3   Reading 快速阅读

Table Manners

There are many differences in table manners across the boundaries. It is really worth your time to learn about how to behave while eating in other countries. Knowledge of table manners will present your international qualifications.

Don't make noises with your mouth. Close your mouth when eating. People make noises because they eat without their mouths closed. When you drink your soup, do not sip it, but swallow it all in one mouthful.

Don't talk with your full mouth. If someone talks to you, wait until your mouth is empty before answering.

Imagining you are eating with someone you have just met. He spits bones onto the table. He wipes his mouth on his sleeve. He rushes for the best piece of food that is served. He does not have good table manners.

Fortunately, most of us eat neatly and are not greedy. These two points are the basic rules of good table manners.

Different cultures of the world have different table customs because of the food served, utensils used or not used and national customs. By knowing and using the table manners of different cultures, we show that we are willing to learn from them. That is a sure way to make friends.

There is not much call for a complete working knowledge of table manners in America today. Many families only gather all at once around the dinner table at holiday feasts, and most restaurants are too casual to require, or even to allow for, more than basic good table manners. If, having dropped his napkin, a diner at a bistro were to attempt to practice proper etiquette by signaling a member of the staff to bring a fresh one, he would probably have to do without a napkin at all. Try as he might to make eye contact and indicate the nature of the problem with a subtle wiggle of the eyebrow and downward flicker of the glance, he is likely to succeed only in causing his date to think he is making a play for the server. Although strict good manners forbid placing a used eating utensil back on the table, the server removing a plate on which a fork has quite properly been positioned "pointing at 11 o'clock" might just plop that item back where it started, making more of a clatter than if the diner had simply done it herself.

From time to time—perhaps at an important business dinner, a romantic date at a luxury restaurant, or a first dinner with the family of the person who may be "the One" — it is necessary to display a more sophisticated knowledge of table etiquettes. This is not difficult, once you have mastered the basics. Anyone armed with his core knowledge and ability to adapt smoothly to the situation at hand will be able to handle even the most formal event. The goal is not, after all, to demonstrate utter mastery of the most arcane details of etiquette (which would be quite difficult considering the wide variations of customs in different cultures and from generation to generation), but rather to behave with graciousness and poise at the table.

Posture

Proper posture at the table is very important. Sit up straight with your arms held near your body. You should neither lean on the back of the chair nor bend forward to place the elbows on the table. It is permissible to lean forward slightly every now and then and press the elbows very lightly against the edge of the table, if it is obvious that you are not using them for support.

Eating Soup

Dip the spoon into the soup, moving it away from the body, until it is about two-thirds full, then sip the liquid (without slurping) from the side of the spoon (without inserting the whole bowl of the spoon into the mouth). The theory behind this is that a diner who scoops the spoon toward himself is more likely to slosh soup onto his lap, although it is difficult to imagine what sort of eater would stroke the spoon so forcefully through the liquid that he creates waves. It is perfectly fine to tilt the bowl slightly again away from the body to get the last spoonful or two of the soup.

Offering Food

Take note, when you are the host of a party, of the way you offer additional servings to your guests. Urging someone to "have another (or a second or third) helping" can be seen as an unpleasant insinuation that the guest has eaten too much. It is best to phrase each offer of food as if the dish has just been brought out for the first time.

"Please Pass the Salt"

The proper response to this very simple request is to pick up both the salt and the pepper and to place them on the table within reach of the person next to you, who will do the same, and so on, until they reach the person who asked for them. They are neither passed hand-to-hand, nor should anyone other than the original requester sprinkle his food when he has the shakers in his possession. The reason for this is that American etiquette is not about efficiency. Often, the most refined action is that which requires the greatest number of steps to carry it out (as in, for example, the zigzag method of handling a fork and knife).

adapt	使适应，改编
arcane	神秘的，不可思议的
bistro	〈俗〉小酒馆，小咖啡店
casual	偶然的，不经意的

clatter	咔嗒声，哗啦声，嘈杂的谈笑声
core	果核，中心，核心
date	约会（对象）
demonstrate	示范，证明，示威
dip	浸，蘸，沾
downward	向下的
efficiency	效率，功效
elbow	肘
etiquette	礼节，礼仪
feast	节日，盛宴，筵席
flicker	扑动，闪烁，颤动
forbid	禁止，不许
forcefully	强有力地，激烈地
glance	一瞥，眼光，匆匆一看
gracious	亲切的，高尚的
greedy	贪吃的，贪婪的，渴望的
insinuation	暗示，暗讽
lap	（坐时的）大腿前部，膝盖下摆
lean	倚靠，倾斜，倾向
mastery	掌握
mouthful	一口，满口
napkin	餐巾，餐巾纸
neatly	整洁地，优美地
pepper	胡椒粉
plop	使掉下，扑通落下
poise	平衡，姿势，镇静
position	安置，决定……的位置
posture	（身体的）姿势，体态
qualification	资格，条件
refined	精制的，优雅的，精确的
romantic	传奇式的，浪漫的

scoop	掘，挖
shaker	摇动者，混合器
signal	打信号，发信号
sip	吸吮
slosh	溅，泼
slurp	啧啧吃，啜食
sophisticated	诡辩的，久经世故的
spit	吐（唾沫），吐出
sprinkle	撒（某物）于（某物之表面），洒
subtle	敏感的，微妙的，精细的
swallow	吞咽
tilt	（使）倾斜，（使）翘起
urge	催促，力劝，极力主张
utensil	器具
utter	全然的，十足的，彻底的
variation	变更，变化，变异
wiggle	踌躇，摆动
wipe	擦，揩
zigzag	曲折的，齿形的，Z形的

Phrases

attempt to	尝试，企图
be armed with	用……武装
be willing to	愿意
carry out	进行，实施
make a noise	制造噪声
make a play for	挖空心思吸引，想尽办法获得
make friends	交朋友
pick up	拾起，捡起
point at	指向

after all	毕竟
at hand	在手边，在附近
from generation to generation	一代代，世世代代
from time to time	有时，不时
in the possession of sb.	为某人所有
now and then	时而，不时

Part 4 Writing 写作技巧

A Letter of Complaints
抱怨及投诉信

Subject: Complaint about a restaurant's service

Dear Mr. Carl,

My wife and I had heard from friends that dining at The Seaside was an enjoyable experience. Therefore, we reserved a table for last Saturday night and invited another couple to join us. Things got off to a shaky start that no table was ready when we arrived. After a 40-minute wait we were finally seated.

The waiter seemed hurried and annoyed. Two of us ordered the vichyssoise and were disappointed. The salmon with crabmeat stuffing fell short of expectations.

Since our guests included my law firm's most important client, I avoided any complaint about the food or confrontation with the irritable waiter, but I'm disappointed nonetheless.

From the reputation you've built, I can only conclude that our experience was an exception. It was, however, enough to keep us from ever returning.

Yours faithfully,

Steve Warner

Writing Practice

Fill in the following complaint letter by translating the Chinese in the brackets.

Dear Mr. Worthington,

_____ (一个令人相当烦恼的方面) of the otherwise satisfactory commuter train service from Lancaster to downtown Manchester is the playing of the radio over the loud speaker system.

This was particularly objectionable this morning on train 610 where riders were subjected to the incessant blaring of KIOU for _____ (几乎全程). Evidently whoever called the stops was unaware that the background noise of his radio accompanied his announcements. _____ (而更糟的是), he apparently forgot to press his off switch, and _____ (一千名乘客被迫聆听) this clatter.

Noise pollution on city buses is usually confined to an individual carrying a loud radio. Old Smoky Railroad does it on a loud radio with a grand scale. I think it should stop.

Yours truly,
Tom Wallace

 Part 5 Vocabulary Expansion 词汇扩展

baked chicken with salt	盐焗鸡
baked lobster with sauce	香汁烤龙虾
bird's nest soup	燕窝汤
braised abalone with mushroom	蘑菇扒鲍鱼
braised duck with brown sauce	酱鸭
braised stuffed duck with salt and pepper	清炖鸭子
deep-fried pork chop	椒盐排骨
egg white puffs with fish slices	芙蓉鱼片
fish slices in vinegar gravy	醋熘鱼片
fish-flavored pork	鱼香肉丝
fragrant crisp duck	香酥鸭
fried Mandarin fish in chilli sauce	干烧鳜鱼
fried shredded cuttlefish	炒鱿鱼丝

grilled beef steak	铁扒牛排
hot and sour soup	酸辣汤
kung po chicken with peanuts	宫保鸡丁
meat balls braised in brown sauce	红烧狮子头
Mongolian beef with ginger sauce	姜汁牛肉
pork slices with gravy	滑熘里脊
roast mutton chop	烤羊排
roast suckling piggy	乳猪拼盘
sautéed shrimp meat	清炒虾仁
sliced chicken with curry sauce	咖喱鸡片
sliced ham and wax gourd soup	火腿冬瓜汤
sliced mutton rinsed in chafing dish	涮羊肉
steamed perch	清蒸鲈鱼
steamed rice flour pork	粉蒸肉
stewed shark's fin in brown sauce	烧鱼翅
sweet and sour pork	糖醋古老肉
tender boiled chicken with soy sauce	白斩鸡
twice cooked pork	回锅肉
wonton egg drop soup	云吞蛋花汤

Unit 6

Communication Service 通信服务

> **Learning objectives 学习目标**
>
> After learning this unit, you should
> - acquire the knowledge about how to answer different kinds of communication service, such as how to make telephone calls, post letters and parcels, etc.;
> - learn the practical knowledge about communication service;
> - find ways to improve your e-mail writing skills.

 Part 1　Background knowledge 背景知识

　　When traveling, people are bound to use some means of communication to send and receive messages, or search for some useful information. Today's communication choices are varied: telephone, mobile phone, mail, e-mail, fax, Internet and more. They are very convenient and have become an indispensable part in people' life.

Types of phones

　　1. Local call (市内电话).

　　2. IDD and DDD: international direct-dialed phone (国际长途直拨电话) and domestic direct-dialed phone (国内长途直拨电话). They are long-distance telephone calls in which the caller dials the number directly without the help of an operator.

Unit 6   Communication Service 通信服务

3. Collect call（对方付费电话）：a telephone call in which the calling party wants to place a call at the called party's expense.

4. Person-to-person call（叫人电话）：an operator assisted call in which the calling party wants to speak to a specific party and not simply to anyone who answers. The caller is not charged for the call unless the requested party can be reached. This method was popular when telephone calls were relatively expensive.

5. Station-to-station call（叫号电话）：a method of placing a telephone call with or without assistance, in which the calling party agrees to talk to whoever answers the telephone.

 Part 2   Speaking 对话训练

Dialogue 1

Making a Telephone Call

(A: Clerk; B: Linda; C: Franklin)

A: ABC Company. Can I help you?

B: Hello! Can I speak to Mr. Franklin?

A: Which Franklin? There are two Franklins here.

B: Tony Franklin, the marketing manager.

A: OK. Just a minute, please. I'll put you through. (After a while) Sorry, Mr. Franklin is not available now. He is having a meeting.

B: Can I leave a message for him?

A: Of course.

B: Could you tell him that Linda Hu from China called him and asked him to call back as soon as possible.

A: What's your number, please?

B: My telephone number is 347-780-7556.

A: OK. Can I confirm the information? Linda Hu from China called and asked Mr. Franklin to call her back as soon as possible. Her telephone number is 347-780-7556. Right?

B: That's right.

A: I've taken them down and I'll let him know, Ms. Hu.

B: Thank you very much. Bye.

A: Bye.

(After some time)

C: Hello, is that Linda?

B: Yes. Who is it? ... Aha, Tony! I recognized your voice right away.

C: Yes. Linda. I just got your message. What a surprise! Didn't you tell me you would come here next week?

B: Yes, but I changed my plan. Tony, I can't believe I got hold of you at last. I tried to contact you by phone several times, but you were not in.

C: I'm sorry. I'm a bit busy recently. Where are you now? Shall we meet after work?

B: Yes, I'm staying at the Time Hotel. We can meet if you are free then.

Unit 6 Communication Service 通信服务

C: Can you find my place? If you can't, I shall be very glad to pick you up.

B: No, thank you. I can find the place. See you then.

C: See you.

Notes

1. available   可用的，可得到的；空闲的
2. the Time Hotel   时代饭店
3. pick up   接送；获得；收拾

Dialogue 2

At the Post Office

(Scene: Bob wants to deliver a parcel to Shanghai. Now he comes to the post office.)

Postal clerk1: Hello, may I help you?

Bob: Yes, I'd like to have this parcel and letter delivered to Shanghai.

Postal clerk1: Oh, we only carry out remittance business. For parcels, please go to the next counter.

Bob: Thank you! … Hello, I have a parcel and a letter to deliver.

Postal clerk2: Where do you want it to be delivered to?

Bob: I want to post it to Shanghai.

Postal clerk2: How would you like to send them?

Bob: I'd like to send them by express.

Postal clerk2: What are inside the parcel?

Bob: They are just some clothes and tea. There's nothing fragile.

Postal clerk2: OK, please fill out this form and indicate the value of the content.

Bob: Sure. What's the postage, please?

Postal clerk2: Hold on, let me put the parcel on the scale. It weighs up to 15 kg, and that will be 217 yuan. The letter is 6 yuan. So it's 223 yuan in total, please.

Bob: Here is 300 yuan.

Postal clerk2: Here is your change and receipt. Please check it.

Bob: Thank you. By the way, can you tell me how long it takes to send the parcel to Shanghai?

Postal clerk2: About 4 days.

Bob: OK. Thanks.

Postal clerk2: You're welcome.

1. deliver a parcel 邮寄包裹
2. remittance business 汇款业务
3. express 快件，特快专递
4. fragile 易碎的
5. indicate 标示，指示，指出
6. postage 邮费，邮资

Part 3　Reading 快速阅读

Social Networking: Mobile Phones

Picture A: A girl goes to college. On the first day she doesn't know anybody in the classroom, but it's OK because she has a mobile phone with her. Only a few clicks and she accesses the profiles of eight students in the classroom, including their pictures. Luckily, two of them come from the same city where she lives. She sends messages to them and they start to chat.

Picture B: An entrepreneur is on the lookout for a new marketing director at a conference. Within minutes, he has identified nine people in the hall with the right CVs. His mobile tells him one of them is standing 15 feet away. That evening, a record of all the people he has met is automatically displayed with their profiles on his home computer.

This is not science fiction. As the blooming of technology development, the explosion in Internet-based social networking (My space, Facebook) could also serve the position of a computer. In fact, many of those applications have already been adapted.

So how does it work? The key is the coming together of Internet-connected mobile phones and location or proximity technology. You can browse the Internet quickly and easily on most new phones. Phones know where they are, thanks to in-built GPS satellite technology from mobile phone masts. They can then tell if other phones are in the same area. Bluetooth short-range radio technology is also standard on most mobiles and with this technology, phones can pick up the presence of other bluetooth-enabled phones within about 20 meters.

Effectively, by linking these two developments, your phone can tell if someone is near you and can access lots of information about them—the perfect ingredients for real social interaction.

The possibilities are endless. Can't you ever put names to faces? Do you want to avoid all accountants, lawyers or journalists? Keep seeing that handsome man at the bar and need a common interest to get the ball rolling. All these scenarios are being solved by the new wave of mobile applications.

One company based in Berlin has just gone live with its mobile social network. More than 3 000 young Germans have signed up to the aka-aki service in just over a month.

Users of the service download an application onto their mobile phones for free. The software uses bluetooth, and when another member's phone comes within range, it pings. The user can then check who it is and choose to access that person's profile, message them and, if they want, go over and have a chat.

Stefanie Hoffman, 30 years old, one of the aka-aki's founders, said that although she met her boyfriend through aka-aki it was not just about dating. "The business applications are real," she said. "I went to a conference the other day—one girl and 80 guys—and usually I would feel very reluctant to go up to someone to talk. But my phone told me there were half a dozen aka-aki members and so I could introduce myself."

That privileged sense of belonging is the key both to the success of mobile social networking and the greatest barrier. People will want to join because they can be part of a connected community. But until enough people join, these mobile networks will not take off. It is probably going to take one of the big beasts of Internet social network such as Facebook, which already has many millions of members, to achieve this.

The other big question mark is privacy. Why would people want total strangers to have access to their details?

In the Mitte district of Berlin, Sehnaz Sensan, 27 years old, is a student and aka-aki member. After I had messaged her to ask if we could talk, she said that she "encountered" mainly men (early adopters of new technology tend to be young men). "I can control what is on my profile and what people can know about me," she said. "They message me to say hello and I can message back and we can meet up or I can ignore it. It is a way of breaking the ice."

What about being bothered by strangers? "Men can come up to you anyway without knowing about you," Ms. Sensan said. "That's much more insulting. If I don't want an encounter, then I don't switch it on."

Michael Arrington, one of the most influential technology bloggers in the world, says that the days when people are not happy to broadcast their CV or personal life electronically are over. "People always trade off privacy for removal of friction," he says. "A few years from now we will use our mobile devices to help us to remember details of people we know. It will help us to meet new people for dating, business and friendship. Using your phone to create or enhance real world interactions is a killer application, but no one has cracked the nut yet. Once it happens, look out."

Arrington has blogged that Apple's hugely successful iPhone would be a great place to start. He has seen an "awesome" application being developed and says that iPhone users are the perfect group for a mobile social network—they are technological, elitist and identified with their brand.

Analysts and commentators are predicting huge growth in the sector. Aka-aki, which was developed from a university diploma project, has serious funding from a leading German venture capitalist.

It is not difficult to see how networks like aka-aki make money. Anyone who has watched the film *Minority Report* with Tom Cruise will have seen how shops could message those on the network with offers when they pass by.

In another scenario, businesses such as restaurants could pay to access the service and when a member walks in, the store's profile appears. The member chooses to add the restaurant to a list of favored brands and next week he receives a two-for-one meal offer. The restaurant gets targeted "permission" advertising and more diners on a slow night.

But in the end are mobile social networks not just a replacement for people simply talking to each other? Roman Hansler, another aka-aki co-founder, says that seeing other people's details on your mobile in real life is conversation-starter, not a replacement. "This is about opening doors for real communication, not sitting in a virtual chat room", he said.

Vocabulary

network	网络，网状系统
click	咔嗒声，咔嚓声；点击
access	进入；访问；存取；接近
entrepreneur	企业家，主办人
identify	识别，鉴别，认出
automatically	自动地，机械地
display	陈列，展览
fiction	小说；虚构；编造
explosion	爆炸，爆发，激增，扩大
proximity	接近，邻近，距离
in-built	内置的；与生俱来的
satellite	卫星；人造卫星
interaction	合作，配合，交互作用
accountant	会计（员）；会计师
scenario	（电影等）剧情说明；描述
ping	发出撞击声；砰地发声
reluctant	不情愿的，勉强的
privileged	保密的；享有特权的
barrier	障碍，隔阂，栅栏
beast	野兽；畜生
encounter	遭遇，偶然碰到，邂逅
insulting	出言不逊的，无礼的
broadcast	广播，播放，传播

electronically	用电子方法；用电子装置
awesome	可怕的，棒极了
elitist	优秀人才的，杰出者的
commentator	评论员，实况广播员
diploma	文凭，毕业证书，执照
capitalist	资本家
permission	允许；许可
co-founder	共同创办人，共同创始人
virtual	实质上的，事实上的

Phrases

be reluctant to	不情愿；勉强
marketing director	营销总监
science fiction	科幻小说
social networking	社交网络
proximity technology	感应技术
the new wave	新一轮
short-range	短程的，短距离的
sense of belonging	归属感
killer application	撒手锏应用
diploma project	毕业设计
venture capitalist	风险投资商
chat room	聊天室
sign up	签约；签署
switch on	开；打开；接通
just around the corner	指日可待；临近
on a slow night	（生意等）清淡的，不忙碌的夜晚
on the lookout	注视着；警惕

Part 4　Writing 写作技巧

E-mail
电子邮件

E-mail usually includes To, Re, Subject, Cc, Bcc and the mail body. In addition, the attachment is also used in writing e-mails, such as photos, letters, etc.

From: "John Smith" johnsmith@hotmail.com
To: "Michael" 12369@yahoo.com
Subject: room reservation
Date: Mon, October 10th, 2020

Hi! Michael,
　　I will go to Beijing next week. If you are not too busy, will you book a single room at the Crown Hotel for me? I'm leaving for Beijing on November 6th and will stay there for one week.
　　I'm looking forward to your reply.
　　Thanks in advance.
John

From: "David" davidwh@126.com
To: "Terrence" Terrencekb25@go2map.com
Subject: tell me your flight number, date and the time

Dear Terrence,
　　I'm glad to hear that you are coming to Shanghai. Have you booked the flight yet? Once you confirm the flight number, date and the expected arrival time, please let me know. I'll pick you up at the airport. See you soon.

Best regards,

David

Useful Expressions

Glad to have got your e-mail from...

Thank you for your e-mail.

Did you receive the e-mail I sent a few days ago?

My new e-mail address is...

I forwarded your e-mail to...

Write back when you get a chance and let me know what's new.

Let me know if you have received the attachment.

Please try to send the attachment again.

Writing Practice

Fill in the following e-mail by translating the Chinese in the brackets.

Dear Mr. Black,

Christmas and New Year are around the corner. We are planning an English party to celebrate them and we would like to invite you to participate. It will be held on December 23, 2020 in the club from 6:30 p.m. to 9:00 p.m. We do hope you can make it as we are looking forward with great pleasure to seeing you. _____ (我已将节目单发在附件里，请查收). By the way, I have a new e-mail address. If you want to contact me, _____ (您可以发邮件至我的新邮箱 Chenhui@sina.com).

Warmest regards,

Chenhui

Part 5 Vocabulary Expansion 词汇扩展

| a room with internet service | 能上网的房间 |
| aerogram | 航空邮件 |

alley	胡同，小巷
country code	国家代码
county	县
declare	说明，申报
desktop computer	台式计算机
directory assistance	电话号码查询服务
envelope	信封
express mail service	特快专递
extension	电话分机
floor（FL/F）	楼层，地板
forward	转递
international code	国际代码
lane	巷
number（NO.）	号码
outside line	外线
palmtop	掌上计算机
parcel service counter	包裹服务柜台
pillar box	邮筒
post office	邮局
printed matter	印刷品
printer	打印机
public phone	公用电话
registered letter	挂号信
return receipt	回执
room（R）	室；房间
special delivery	限时专递
stamps counter	邮票售卖处
street（St.）/ road（Rd.）/boulevard（Blvd.）	街、路、大道
surcharge	附加费
surfing	（互联网上）冲浪

telephone book	电话号码簿
telephone booth	电话亭
township/city/district	乡、镇/市/区
urgent	紧急的
yellow page	黄页
zip code	邮政编码

Unit 7

Meeting Service 会议服务

Learning objectives 学习目标

After learning this unit, you should

- acquire the knowledge about meeting service;
- organize the basic words and expressions about meeting service;
- learn some cultural knowledge about meeting service;
- find ways to improve your writing skills in booking form for conference rooms;
- be familiar with business English and holding meetings in English.

Part 1 Background knowledge 背景知识

Meeting service means that agents and operators provide the service in meeting planning, organizing, inspecting, reception and supporting.

The overall meeting service 整体会议服务

Before the meeting

(1) To communicate with the conference organizer (telephone/Internet/interview);

(2) To develop a comprehensive meeting plan (A/B/C/...) and provide reasonable recommendations;

(3) To help customers study;

(4) To determine the program (nature/request/schedule);

(5) To submit budget;

(6) To sign the contract and pay a deposit;

(7) To book hotel/session sites/vehicles according to the requests;

(8) To prepare meeting articles, including representative cards/emblems/meeting data/pens and papers/souvenirs, etc.;

(9) To arrange the meeting place: welcome brands/banners/signs/testing equipment;

(10) Pre-negotiation.

In the meeting

(1) Pre-prepared: the required meeting information/conference articles/meeting speeches/other related items in place;

(2) Meeting place: hotels/conference rooms/welcome banners or signs in place;

(3) Conference equipment preparation: laptop/projector/lighting/sound/recording equipment in place;

(4) Shuttle service: the transportation from airport and station by cars/formal services;

(5) Meeting registration: on behalf of the permit process/fees/hard material and so on;

(6) Accommodation: responsible for the distribution of rooms;

(7) Conference dining: the dining and banquet arrangements;

(8) Conference entertainment: entertainment forms/consumption standards/confirmation of entertainment sites;

(9) Other meeting services: photos and DVs/public relations/secretarial service/translation and related service;

(10) Tickets: offering return air tickets/booking service of train tickets;

(11) Logistics and external coordination.

After the meeting

(1) Travel arrangements after the meeting;

(2) Checkout: setting out the cost in the process of meeting details and check out;

(3) Data: data collection, according to the customer's requests to produce contact or meeting roster;

(4) Feedback of the customer/follow-up service;

(5) To sum up the meeting.

 Part 2 Speaking 对话训练

Dialogue 1

Booking a Booth

(R: Reservation Clerk; C: Client)

R: Good morning, Zara Exhibition Center. May I help you?

C: Yes, please. I'd like to register the International Motorcycle Exhibition.

R: May I have your name, sir?

C: I'm Thomas Brown.

R: Let me check, Mr. Brown. Sorry for keeping you waiting. Fortunately, there are still some booths available. If you send us your registration form and registration fees within two weeks, it's still possible for you to get one booth.

C: May I register a booth now on the phone?

R: Sure. Which credit card would you like to use?

C: American Express.

R: Fine. I'm glad to help you sign up on the phone. Perhaps you can answer me some questions to start with?

C: Sure.

R: May I know your phone number, e-mail and your company's name?

C: My phone number is 867932294, my e-mail is thomasbrown@dola.com and my company's full name is Dola Motorcycle Assembling Corporation.

R: Mr. Thomas Brown at 867932294 is from Dola Motorcycle Assembling Corporation, and your e-mail is thomasbrown@dola.com. Is it right?

C: Yes.

R: Are you looking for a standard package booth or non-standard one?

C: What is the charge for each one?

R: The nine-square-meter booth costs at least $23,000 per unit while the six-square-meter booth costs at least $17,000 per unit. Which one would you prefer?

C: One nine-square-meter booth, please.

R: Where do you expect to be located?

C: Can I reserve a space in the center?

R: Sorry but all center booths are booked up. We have only corner booths left.

C: Oh, that's fine. I'll take a corner booth.

R: There is a corner booth next to the right of the entrance. Will that be all right?

C: OK, I'll take it.

R: Thank you, Mr. Brown. You have reserved one nine-square-meter corner booth to the right of the entrance. The booth number is A-022. May I have your credit card number?

C: The number is 845319400327 and expiration date is 31/12/2036.

R: Thanks. I'll send you a letter to confirm your reservation soon. Anything else I can do for you?

C: No, thank you very much. Goodbye!

R: Thanks for calling. Goodbye!

1. booth   货摊；公用电话亭
2. credit card   信用卡
3. American Express   美国运通卡
4. standard package booth   标准包价摊位
5. non-standard package booth   非标准包价摊位

Dialogue 2

Venue Reservation

(C: Clerk of Conference Service Center; S: Mr. Smith)

C: Good morning, Mountain Hotel, Conference Service Center. Mary speaking. May I help you?

S: This is Eric Smith from Smile Company. I'd like to reserve a convention room in your hotel.

C: Certainly. What size of conference room do you have in mind?

S: For about one which can contain 150 people. We're holding a press conference from 5:00 p.m. to 7:00 p.m., and a cocktail party from 7:00 p.m. to 9:30 p.m.

C: Which seating style would you prefer for the press conference?

S: Theatre style, please.

C: Sure. May I know the time and date, please?

S: Our plan is on Sunday in November. What's your suggestion?

C: Just a minute, Mr. Smith. I'll check the reservation record. Thanks for your waiting. What about in late November? That is November 16th or 23rd.

S: November 23rd, please. What facilities do you offer with the room?

C: The convention room is equipped with three cable microphones, one LED projector with screen, laptop connection and wireless network access.

S: Great! What's the price?

C: We have two convention rooms for your choice. One is 150 m^2 at 1,980 yuan per night and the other is 200 m^2 at 2,480 yuan per night. The latter one is more luxurious and spacious. Which one would you prefer?

S: The latter one, please. Does the rate include the furniture?

C: Yes. Would you like to make a guaranteed reservation with your credit card?

S: All right. Do you accept Visa?

C: Yes, may I know the number?

S: It's 9934256.

C: 9934256. May I have your passport number?

S: A20395.

C: A20395. Thank you. Let me repeat your reservation: a conference room for Mr. Eric Smith, at 2,480 yuan per night, on Sunday, November 23rd, from 5:00 p.m. to 9:30 p.m. Is that right?

S: Yes.

C: My name is Mary Wong. Please just call me if there is anything I can help. Thank you for calling me and we look forward to serving you.

S: Thank you. See you.

C: See you.

1. conference service center 会议服务中心
2. have in mind 考虑；想到
3. press conference 新闻发布会
4. cable microphone 有线话筒
5. spacious 广阔的；宽敞的
6. latter 后面的，较后的

Part 3   Reading 快速阅读

Holding Meetings in English

One of the most common requirements of business English is holding meetings in English. The following sections provide some useful languages and phrases for conducting meetings and making contributions to a meeting. Meetings generally follow a more or less similar structure and can be divided into the following parts.

1. Introduction

- Opening the meeting

Unit 7 Meeting Service 会议服务

- Welcoming and introducing participants
- Stating the principal objectives of a meeting
- Giving an apology for someone who is absent

2. Reviewing Past Business

- Reading the minutes (notes) of the last meeting
- Dealing with recent developments

3. Beginning the Meeting

- Introducing the agenda
- Allocating roles (secretary, participants)
- Agreeing on the ground rules for the meeting (contributions, timing, decision-

making, etc.)

4. Discussing Items

- Introduction of the first item on the agenda
- Closing an item
- Next item
- Giving control to the next participant

5. Finishing the Meeting

- Summarizing
- Finishing up
- Suggesting and agreeing on time, date and place for the next meeting
- Thanking participants for their attendances
- Closing the meeting

The following sentences and phrases are used to conduct a meeting. They are useful if you are called on to conduct a meeting.

1. Opening

Good morning/afternoon, everyone.

If we are all here, let's get started/start the meeting/start.

2. Welcoming and Introducing

Please join me in welcoming (name of participant).

We're pleased to welcome (name of participant).

I'd like to extend a warm welcome to (name of participant).

It's a pleasure to welcome (name of participant).

I'd like to introduce (name of participant).

3. Stating the Principal Objectives

We're here today to...

I'd like to make sure that we...

Our main aim today is to...

I've called this meeting in order to...

4. Giving an Apology for Someone Who is Absent

I'm afraid (name of participant) cannot be with us today. She is in...

Unfortunately, (name of participant) will not be with us today because he...

I have received an apology for absence from (name of participant).

5. Reading the Minutes (Notes) of the Last Meeting

To begin with, I'd like to quickly go through the minutes of our last meeting.

First, let's go over the report from the last meeting which was held on (date).

Here are the minutes from our last meeting which was on (date).

6. Dealing with Recent Developments

Jack, can you tell us how the X project is progressing?

John, have you completed the report on the new accounting package?

Has everyone received a copy of the State Foundation Report on current marketing trends?

7. Moving Forward

If there is nothing else we need to go over, let's move on to today's agenda.

Shall we get down to business?

If there are no further developments, I'd like to move on to today's agenda.

8. Introducing the Agenda

Have you all received a copy of the agenda?

There are X items on the agenda. First ... second ... third ... last...

Shall we take the points in this order?

If you don't mind, I'd like to go in order today.

I suggest we take Item 2 at last.

9. Allocating Roles (secretary, participants)

(Name of participant) has agreed to take the minutes.

(Name of participant) has kindly agreed to give us a report on...

(Name of participant) will lead Point 1, (name of participant) Point 2, and (name of participant) Point 3.

(Name of participant), would you mind taking notes today?

10. Agreeing on the Ground Rules for the Meeting (contributions, timing, decision-making, etc.)

We will first hear a short report on each point, followed by a discussion of…

I suggest we go round the table first.

Let's make sure we finish by…

I'd suggest we…

There will be five minutes for each item.

We'll have to keep each item in 15 minutes. Otherwise we'll never get through.

11. Introducing the First Item on the Agenda

So, let's start with…

I'd suggest we start with…

Why don't we start with…?

So, the first item on the agenda is…

Peter, would you like to kick off?

Shall we start with…?

(Name of participant), would you like to introduce this item?

12. Closing an Item

Shall we leave that item until…

Why don't we move on to…?

If nobody has anything else to add, let's…

13. Next Item

Let's move on to the next item.

Now that we've discussed X, let's now…

The next item on today's agenda is…

Now we come to the question of…

14. Giving Control to the Next Participant

I'd like to hand over to (name of participant) who is going to lead the next point.

Next, (name of participant) is going to take us through…

Now, I'd like to introduce (name of participant) who is going to…

15. Summarizing

Before we close today's meeting, let me just summarize the main points.

Let me quickly go over today's main points. To sum up…

OK, why don't we quickly summarize what we've done today?

In brief…

Shall I go over the main points?

16. Finishing Up

Right, it looks as though we've covered the main items.

If there are no other comments, I'd like to wrap this meeting up.

Let's bring this to a close for today.

17. Suggesting and Agreeing on Time, Date and Place for the Next Meeting

Shall we set the date for the next meeting?

So, the next meeting will be on … (day), the … (date) of … (month) at (place)…

Let's make our next meeting on … (day), the … (date) of … (month) at (place)…

What about the following Wednesday? How is that?

18. Thanking Participants for their Attendances

I'd like to thank Marianne and Jeremy for coming over from London.

Thank you all for attending.

Thanks for your participation.

19. Closing the Meeting

The meeting is finished. We'll see each other next…

The meeting is closed.

I declare the meeting closed.

Vocabulary

agenda	议程
allocate	分配
appropriate	适当的
conduct	行为，操行；引导，管理
contribution	捐献，贡献
generally	一般，通常
introduction	介绍，导言，绪论
minute	备忘录，笔记，摘录
objective	目标；客观的

participant	参与者
principal	负责人；校长；主要的
requirement	要求；必要条件
review	回顾，复习
section	部分，项，区
similar	相似的，类似的
situation	情形；（建筑物等的）位置
state	声明，陈述，规定
summarize	概述，总结，摘要而言

Phrases

decision-making	决策
recent development	近期动态
ground rules	基本原则；基本准则
the minutes of a meeting	会议纪要
the principal objectives	会议主要议题
warm welcome	热烈欢迎
agree on	达成一致
close an item	结束一个议题
close the meeting	宣布散会
conduct a meeting	组织会议
divide into	分成
finish up	结束；完成；用光
give apology for	道歉
give control to	请……发言
hold a meeting	主持会议
move forward/on to sth.	转向下一个议题
open the meeting	宣布会议开始
run a meeting	主持会议
more or less	或多或少

Part 4　Writing 写作技巧

Memo
内部通知

Memo is short for memorandum, and it is a kind of official document. It is used to describe the standard format of internal communication, which an organization uses for its own staff. A memo may pass on information, explain new procedures, announce changes, make requests, confirm results or offer advice. In addition, memos are rarely sent to other organizations.

Memo

To: Department Managers and Secretaries

Cc: Personnel Manager and Secretary

From: John Parson, General Manager

Date: April 20, 2021

Re: New Procedure for New Staff Registration

Effective from June 1, new procedure will be implemented in the Personnel Office to ensure that new staff registration will be handled quickly.

After that date, new staff must fill out the new registration form (Form WR-152). Copies of this new form will be available in the Personnel Office next week.

All the department managers and secretaries are asked to assist new staff to complete the new form. Address any questions concerning this new procedure to me at 8808 or to Susan, my secretary, at 8809, or to my e-mail box at parson@virtual.com.

Best regards,
John Parson

Writing Practice

You are the manager of a company. Your company/department is going to arrange a two-day fall outing soon. Write a memo to inform the staff concerning with the time, place, itinerary, charge, and everything else necessary.

Part 5　Vocabulary Expansion 词汇扩展

advisory committee	顾问委员会，咨询委员会
assembly	大会
banquet	酒宴
board of directors	董事会
box supper	慈善餐会
closing ceremony	闭幕式
closing speech	闭幕词
closure	闭幕
cocktail party	鸡尾酒会
congress	代表大会
fancy ball	化装舞会
farewell party	欢送会
general committee	总务委员会
notice board	布告牌
opening ceremony	开幕式
opening	开幕
other business	其他事项
plenary meeting	全会
procedure	程序
public gallery	旁听席
rules of procedure	议事规则
secretariat	秘书处
session	会期，会议期间

speaker	报告人
deliver a speech	做报告
place on the agenda	列入议程
welcome meeting	欢迎会

Unit 8

Recreation and Entertainment 休闲娱乐服务

Learning objectives 学习目标

After learning this unit, you should
- learn what is and how to give information about recreation and entertainment;
- organize the basic words and expressions about travel recreation and entertainment;
- acquire some cultural knowledge about recreation and entertainment;
- find ways to improve your writing skills in thank-you letters;
- be familiar with some domestic famous places and ways of recreation and entertainment.

 Part 1　Background knowledge 背景知识

Types of recreation 休闲娱乐服务的种类

After a busy sightseeing day, we may be exhausted physically, yet excited mentally. Therefore, during the process of our tour, the travel agency usually arranges some leisure time when we can participate in some activities which may consume less energy, such as playing golf, going to famous local bars, enjoying and appreciating traditional Chinese opera, going to the cinema, and so on.

 Part 2   Speaking 对话训练

Dialogue 1

In the Fitness Center

(W: Waiter; D: Daphne, a guest)

W: Welcome to the gym. Can I help you?

D: I'd like to take some exercise. Could you tell me what facilities you have here?

W: Certainly, madam. We have a well-equipped gym with all the latest recreational sports apparatus—exercise bicycles, weights, swimming pools, tennis courts—that sort of things. Basically there are two types: the ones for aerobics and the others for strengthening your muscles.

D: OK, thank you very much. But I heard that intense exercise can hurt your muscles.

W: Well, that depends on how you do it. Some people want to be in shape in a short time, so they overstress their bodies and can get hurt that way. But if you take it slowly and you won't.

D: But it seems that other forms of exercise can also achieve these results.

W: Yes, they can. But in the gymnasium you have all the right equipment for different parts of your body. You can work on only your abdomen, biceps or triceps, or just build up your stamina.

D: So professional! Well, may I try to run on the treadmill?

W: Of course. This way, please.

Notes

1. recreational　　　　　　娱乐的，消遣的
2. apparatus　　　　　　　装置；器官
3. aerobics　　　　　　　　有氧运动法
4. strengthen　　　　　　　加强；变坚固
5. muscle　　　　　　　　　肌肉
6. overstress　　　　　　　使……受力过大
7. gymnasium　　　　　　　体育馆；健身房
8. abdomen　　　　　　　　腹部
9. biceps　　　　　　　　　肱二头肌
10. triceps　　　　　　　　肱三头肌
11. stamina　　　　　　　　毅力；精力；持久力
12. professional　　　　　　专业的；职业的
13. treadmill　　　　　　　踏车，跑步机

Dialogue 2

Swimming

(W: Waiter; G: Gavin, a guest)

W: Good afternoon, sir. May I help you?

G: I'd like to have a good figure. What kind of exercise do you suggest?

W: Just a good figure? Don't you want to have good health, too?

G: Can I have both?

W: Sure. Swimming is the best exercise to achieve both goals.

G: Why?

W: Because you can exercise your whole body. It is also good for muscle development and stamina.

G: I'm just new to swim. And I'm not good at swimming.

W: Don't worry about it. You can make a practice in the shallow area of the pool at first, the life guard nearby is getting ready to help you whenever you need.

G: How about the temperature of the water?

W: 29℃ and we change the water every other day.

G: That's good. I'll have a try.

Notes

1. shallow area   浅水区

2. life guard   救生员

3. temperature   温度

Unit 8　Recreation and Entertainment 休闲娱乐服务

Part 3　Reading 快速阅读

Peking Opera

Beijing opera or Peking opera is a kind of Chinese opera which arose in the mid-19th century and was extremely popular in the Qing Dynasty court. It is widely regarded as one of the cultural treasures of China. Beijing and Tianjin are regarded as the base cities of Peking opera in the north while Shanghai is the base in the south.

Although it is called Beijing opera, its origins are not in Beijing but in the Chinese provinces of Hubei and Anhui. Beijing opera gets its two main melodies, Xipi and Erhuang, from Hubei and Anhui operas. Many dialogues are also carried out in an archaic dialect originated partially from those regions. It also absorbed music and arias from other operas and musical arts such as the historic Qinqiang as well as being very and was strongly influenced by Kunqu, the form that preceded it as the court art. It is regarded that Beijing opera came into being when the Four Great Anhui Troupes came to Beijing in 1790. In 1928, some famous Hubei troupes came to Beijing. They often jointly performed in the stage with Anhui troupes. The combination gradually formed Beijing opera's main melodies. Beijing opera was originally staged for the court and came into the public later.

There are four main roles in Peking opera: Sheng（生，male role）, Dan（旦，female role）, Jing（净，painted face, male role）, Chou（丑，clown role）. The three roles other than the second one represent male characters. There is an explanation about why the roles take the names above. It is said that they were chosen to have opposite

109

meanings to their Chinese characters. Sheng in Chinese may mean "strange" or "rare", but the chief male role is a well-known character. Dan, which means "morning" or "masculine", is contrary to the feminine nature of the characters. Jing means "clean", but in fact the paintings on their faces make the characters look unclean but colorful. And Chou in Chinese sometimes represents the animal "ox", which in some senses, is slow and silent—in contrast, the Chou characters are usually quick and talkative.

Facial makeup in Beijing opera is a national cosmetic with special features. As each historical figure or a certain type of person has a certain type of facial makeup, just like we should sing and perform according to the score, they are called "types of facial makeup in operas". It is reported to have originated from mask.

The types of facial makeup in Peking opera are based on a certain personality, temperament or some special types of figures for the use of certain colors. Red facial makeup expresses the warriors of strong persona in operas such as Guan Yu, Jiang Wei, Chang Yuchun; black ones in operas are people with the characters of integrity, bravery and even reckless, such as Bao Zheng, Zhang Fei, and Li Kui; yellow ones represent vicious brutality, such as Yuwen Chengdu and Dian Wei; blue or green ones represent irritable characters, such as Dou Ambassador, Ma Wu; white ones symbolize general treacherous court officials, such as Cao Cao and Zhao Gao.

The color painting methods of facial makeup in Peking opera are basically divided into three categories: kneaded face, smeared face and thickened face. The initial role of facial makeup in opera is to facilitate the development of the plot and personage's personality and psychological characteristics by exaggerating the role with striking appearance. Later types of facial makeup in opera become more complex, delicate, and profound. Facial makeup itself becomes a national pictorial art which manifests facial expressions.

absorb	吸收
Dou Ambassador	窦尔敦
archaic	古老的，陈旧的

aria	唱腔
brutality	残忍，野蛮的行为
complex	复杂的，合成的，综合的
cosmetic	化妆品
court	宫廷，朝廷
facilitate	使容易，使便利，帮助，促进
feminine	女性的
figure	轮廓；图形；数字；表示
irritable	易怒的，急躁的
manifest	表明，证明
masculine	男性的，男子气概的
melody	旋律，曲调
origin	起源，由来；出身，血统
originate	因其，发起，起源，发生
partially	部分地
persona	人，戏剧中的角色
physiological	生理学的，生理学上的
precede	领先（于），在……之前
present	赠给；呈现；提出
profound	深刻的，意义深远的，渊博的
psychological	心理（上）的
reckless	不计后果的
represent	表现；象征；提出异议
score	乐谱
symbolize	象征，作为……的象征
temperament	气质，性情
treacherous	背叛的，奸诈的
treasure	财宝，财富；珍惜；珍藏
troupe	剧团
vicious	不道德的，堕落的，恶意的
warrior	战士，勇士，武士，战斗的

be regarded as	把……看作……
originate from	起源于
contrary to	与……相反
in contrast	相反

kneaded face	揉脸
smeared face	抹脸
thickened face	勾脸

Part 4 Writing 写作技巧

Thank-you Letter
感谢信

A formal thank-you letter should:

(1) express the gratitude;

(2) appreciate the hospitality;

(3) wish to return the favor;

(4) extend thanks again.

Dear Mrs. Lee,

　　I am writing on behalf of our delegation to thank you for your kindness and hospitality extended to us on our visit to London last month. We are extremely grateful to you for all the trouble you took to make our stay in London as comfortable and interesting as possible. In fact, I can assure you that those five days in London were the highlight of our UK tour. We were able to visit the National Rivers Authority, the Town Planning Department of the Engineering School, and several other places of great interest. Also, we were very well taken care of—staying in the Lord Mayor's Mansion House with good food everyday! We could not thank you adequately for all you have done for us.

It will be my privilege and pleasure to return your hospitality sometime in the future when you come to visit us.

Please accept our thanks once again. We look forward to hosting you in China.

Yours respectfully,

Chen Yu

Writing Practice

You just came back to China from your Canadian trip. During your one-week stay, you had a cordial reception. Your successful visit has contributed a lot to your future research. Write a formal thank-you letter to your host to extend your gratitude for the hospitality and help.

Part 5　Vocabulary Expansion　词汇扩展

运动和兴趣爱好名称

amateur dramatic	业余戏剧表演
baseball	棒球
boxing	拳击
cooking	烹饪
cricket	板球
gardening	园艺
golf	高尔夫
horse riding	赛马
knitting	编织
motor racing	赛车

painting	绘画
rugby	英式橄榄球
sailing	帆船
sewing	缝纫
shooting	射击
squash	壁球
track and field	田径
wrestling	摔跤

旅游词汇

China's category A travel agency	一类旅行社
China's category B travel agency	二类旅行社
China's category C travel agency	三类旅行社
clothes, bearing and appearance	服装仪表
guide book	旅游指南
guide practice	导游实践
international tourism	国际旅游
itinerary	旅游计划，旅游线路
local guide	地方导游
local tourist organization	地方旅游组织，地接社
minimum tour price	最低旅游价格
multilingual guide	会多种语言的导游
national guide	全陪，全程导游
national tourist organization	全国旅游组织
low season/off season/off-peak season/season-low/slack season	淡季
on season/peak season/season-high/selling season	旺季
shoulder period/shoulder season	平季
provincial tourism administration	省旅游局
municipal tourism administration	市旅游局
county tourism administration	县旅游局

autonomous prefecture tourism administration	自治州旅游局
autonomous region tourism administration	自治区旅游局
receiving country	旅游接待国
regional tourist organization	区域旅游组织
sightseeing	游览
state-list famous historical and culture cities	国家级历史文化名城
tour arrangement	旅游安排
tour brochure	旅游小册子
tour catalog	旅游团目录
tour code number	旅游代号编码
tour escort/tour conductor/tour director	旅游团陪同
tour leader	领队，团长
tour route	旅游路线
tour talker	自动导游磁带机
touring club	旅游俱乐部
touring	游览
tourism activities	旅游活动
tourism association	旅游协会
tourism authority/tourism office/tourism administration	旅游局
tourism circles	旅游界
tourism council	旅游委员会
tourism destination area	旅游目的地地区
tourism destination country	旅游目的国
tourism destination	旅游目的地
tourism map	旅游地图
tourism periodical	旅游周刊
tourism spots	旅游点
tourism	旅游业，旅游
tourist	游客
travel business/travel operation	旅游业务
travel expert	旅游专家

travel journalist	旅游记者
travel press	旅游报纸
travel publication	旅游出版物
travel writer	旅游作家
travel industry/tourism industry	旅游业
traveling expense	旅费
World Tourism Day	世界旅游日
World Tourism Organization	世界旅游组织

Unit 9

Check-out Service 退房服务

Learning objectives 学习目标

After learning this unit, you should

- learn how to ask and offer information about check-out at a hotel;
- be familiar with the procedures of settling bills;
- organize the basic words and expressions used during check-out;
- acquire some knowledge about check-out;
- find ways to improve your notes writing skills.

Part 1 Background knowledge 背景知识

An Introduction to Check-out at a Hotel 退房服务概述

Check-out is one of the primary tasks of front desk affair. Guests can check out at the cashier of the front desk. Check-out time varies from one hotel to another. In most cases, check-out time at the latest is 12:00 noon or 1:00 p.m. If the guest leaves after the time, he or she will have to pay half or full of the room rate. It is important to set proper check-out time when the guest is about to check out. As many tourists set off at about 8:00 a.m. or 9:00 a.m., they may have to queue for check-out. Therefore, if the guest would like to settle the bill during that time, he or she must allow enough time to do it. However, if the guest notifies the front desk about the departure time beforehand, the clerk may get the bill ready. Thus it will save the guest much time when he or she checks out.

When checking out, the guest can either pay in cash or by credit card or with a traveler's check. If the guest checks out by credit card or with a traveler's check, he or she will be informed to sign the name.

If the guest needs help to take the baggage to the lobby, he or she may call the bellboy counter. The bellboy will come to the room to take the baggage. But do not forget to tip him. If the guest wants the hotel to deposit the valuables or the baggage, he or she can ask the front desk for help. Most hotels provide this free service.

Before paying the bill, the guest must check each item carefully in case there are some mistakes. If the guest disagrees with the bill, he or she can ask the cashier to explain or revise it.

Unit 9　Check-out Service　退房服务

Part 2　Speaking 对话训练

Dialogue 1

Checking Out

(A：Clerk A；B：Nancy Baker, a guest；C：Bellboy；D：Clerk D)

A：Good morning. May I help you?

B：Yes. I'm leaving right now. Could you send a bellboy to take the baggage for me?

A：Of course. Which room are you in?

B：Room 425.

A：All right. The bellboy will be right there.

B：Thank you. (After a while)

C：Bellboy.

B：Come in, please.

C：Good morning, madam. What can I do for you?

119

B: Could you please take the baggage for me? I have three pieces of baggage.

C: OK. I'll take them down to the lobby.

B: Thank you. (Soon they come to the lobby.)

C: Madam. Shall I leave the baggage here?

B: Yes, thank you very much. (She gives tips to check out.)

C: Thanks. (Then Mrs. Baker comes to the front desk to check out.)

B: Hello. I'd like to check out now. I'm Room 425. Can I have my bill now?

D: Of course. Your name, please?

B: Nancy Baker.

D: One moment, please. (The clerk checks it in the computer.) So you stayed here for two nights. This is your bill 960 yuan. Please check it.

B: Does it include service charge and tax?

D: Yes, that's everything. (Mrs. Baker checks it carefully.)

B: OK. Exactly. Do you accept credit card?

D: Certainly. May I have your card, please?

B: Here you are.

D: (The clerk takes an imprint of it.) Mrs. Baker, please sign your name here.

B: Oh, yes.

D: Thanks. Here is your card, bill and receipt. Please take care of them. Hope you have a nice trip and hope to see you soon.

B: Thanks. Bye.

D: My pleasure. Bye.

Notes

1. baggage   包裹
2. tip   小费
3. imprint   印，印记，特征；痕迹

Dialogue 2

Explaining the Bill

(C: Clerk; G: Guest)

C: Good morning, sir. What can I do for you?

G: I'd like to check out. My name is Jack Brown.

C: OK, Mr. Brown. Could you tell me your room number?

G: Room 3308. May I see the bill?

C: Of course, sir. One moment while I print out your bill. Here you are. The total amount is 2,508 yuan. Please have a check.

G: (Check the bill)... I'm sorry. What's this charge of 245 yuan? Could you explain it to me?

C: Sure. That's a 10 percent service charge.

G: Oh, OK. And what's this for?

C: That's for the taxi you called to the World Exposition.

G: Oh, I see. Can I pay in U. S. dollars?

C: No, sir. I'm sorry. But you can get your money changed at the Foreign Exchange Counter in our hotel.

G: Then would credit card be all right?

C: What kind of cards are you holding, sir? We only accept Visa, MasterCard, American Express, and Diners Club.

G: American Express.

C: That's fine. Here is your bill and receipt, sir. We are glad you enjoyed your stay with us and hope you have a nice trip home.

G: Thank you.

Notes

1. total	总计，总数
2. World Exposition	世界博览会
3. Foreign Exchange Counter	外币兑换台
4. Visa, MasterCard, American Express, Diners Club	维萨，万事达，美国运通，大莱卡（信用卡名）

Part 3　Reading 快速阅读

How Hotels Help Themselves to Your Money

If you think your hotel is done with you when you check out, think again. It might just be getting started.

Charges can be quietly added to your hotel bill after you've left. And increasingly, they are.

Unit 9　Check-out Service 退房服务

When Andrew Fox was a weekly guest at a W Hotels & Resorts property, the items he found on his credit card bill after check-out were often bogus—a candy bar he hadn't eaten or a bottle of water he hadn't drunk. Although he successfully fought to have the charges reversed, "It got to the point that before I checked in, I would ask them to remove the goodie-box from my room," he says.

Just a year ago, about one in two hundreds bills at full-service hotels was revised after check-out, according to Bjorn Hanson, an associate professor at New York University. Today, as hotels struggle with slipping occupancy levels and flat-lining growth, properties are wasting no opportunity to add late charges. As a result, the number of re-billings has doubled.

The late charges are usually correct, say experts. And if they are not, most hotels are quick to correct the error, but not always. Some properties either resist crediting their customers or refuse. That's what happened to Charles Garnar when he stayed at the Renaissance Fort Lauderdale Hotel recently. "When we checked out, we were told there were no charges so we had a zero balance," he remembers. But when he returned home after a cruise vacation, he found an unwelcome surprise on his credit card statement: a $57 charge. "It took two days to get through to the accounts payable department," he says. "They said we used the mini-bar."

The hotel only removed the charges after he proved it couldn't have been his. How? Garnar had turned down the mini-bar key when he checked in.

This shouldn't be happening, of course. The latest hotel accounting systems let you see your room charges in real time, often from your TV screen. There's no reason the bill that's slipped under the door on the morning of your check-out shouldn't include all of your charges, with the possible exception of your breakfast check. "It should be your final bill," says Robert Mandelbaum, a hotel expert with PKF Consulting.

In Depth

I contacted several hotel chains to find out about their policy on late charges, including Marriott (which owns the Renaissance) and W Hotels. Only one of the major hotels, InterContinental, bothered to respond. My favorite non-answer came from W, where a spokeswoman told me that, "because of transitions in the company, we don't have an appropriate spokesperson to speak on this topic right now."

Oh, too bad.

Here's what InterContinental, which owns the Crowne Plaza, Holiday Inn and Staybridge Suites, had to say about late billing. It's rare, and usually only happens when guests choose the express check-out option—that's where the bill is slipped under your door on the day of check-out. If someone bills something to your room after 3 a.m., chances are you'll get a late charge.

Normally, guests aren't notified about the charges, because they've agreed to them as part of the terms of their express check-out. But when there's a significant additional fee, a hotel typically notifies travelers before billing them. What if they disagree with the bill? Contact the hotel and tell a representative you have a problem with the charge, recommends by InterContinental spokesman Brad Minor.

"Our hotels value our guests and we want to make sure guests are satisfied with all aspects of their stay," he says.

I'm pretty confident that the other hotels would have said more or less the same thing. But guests don't necessarily agree with that. After I posted Fox's story on my blog, I received a firestorm of comments accusing the hotels of deliberately charging guests after their stay.

It doesn't really matter. What matters is that you, the guest, don't get shocked with a surprise charge on your credit card days or weeks after your vacation. Here are three excuses hotels use for separating you from your money after you've long gone. You might hear some of these reasons articulated by a hotel employee—other excuses are probably reserved for the privacy of the break room or the hotel's executive offices.

Are you sure you didn't take something from the mini-bar?

A vast majority of late check-out charges—about 75 percent, according to Hanson—are from those little refrigerators stocked with vastly overpriced snacks. Hotel mini-bars have become figurative traps that guests get stuck in. Often, they don't even know about it until it's too late. The newest mini-bars have sensors that charge your room the moment an item is moved. In general, some guests would fall into one of these traps at a Los Angeles hotel.

The solution? Don't accept the key to your mini-bar. If there's no key, ask to have the mini-bar (or goody-basket) removed. It's the only way to be sure.

But you checked out before we could charge you!

Unless you're talking about breakfast on the day you check out, this is an empty excuse. Remember, most hotel accounting systems are lightning-fast. The moment you sign your check for an activity or meal, your account is charged. But if a major charge shows up on your credit card, it's worth calling the hotel.

The solution? Review your bill before checking out to make sure nothing is missing. And check out your credit card bill after your stay to make sure nothing is added.

We didn't think you would notice.

I have no proof, no memos or transcripts, scheming hotel employees saying this. Scores of guest experiences suggest this attitude is pervasive behind the front desk. For example, Eugene Santhin, who was a frequent business traveler from Mt. Laurel, New Jersey, before retiring, says he was often billed for water and mini-bar items that weren't consumed. "Many properties charged for breakfast when it was included in the room rate," he adds. To their credit, the hotels quickly removed the items when he protested. But it was the speed with which they did so that made him suspicious. Were they adding these extras to his bill, hoping he wouldn't notice? It's difficult to say for certain.

The solution? Pay attention! Your hotel may be trying to pull a fast one, despite its denials. Keep all of your receipts.

Not all late billings hurt hotel guests. Reader Kate Trabue remembers a recent stay at the InterContinental Sydney where she was hit with unexpected room charges after she checked out. "A call to the billing department got the charges reversed without a problem," she remembers. "The interesting part of this transaction was that because of the exchange rate, I was credited more dollars than the original charge."

accounting	会计；记账；清算账目
accuse	控告，谴责，非难
articulate	用关节连接，接合；清晰明白地说

Unit 9 Check-out Service 退房服务

aspect	（问题等的）方面；外表，方位
associate	副的，合伙的
attitude	态度，看法，意见；姿势
bill	账单，钞票，票据，清单，法案
bogus	假的，伪造的
chain	链（条），镣铐，一连串，一系列；连锁
comment	评论，意见，批评
confident	确信的，肯定的；有信心的，自信的
consulting	商议的，顾问资格的，咨询的
consume	消耗，消费，耗尽
credit	信任，信用，声望，荣誉
	相信，信任；把……记入贷方，存入（账户）
cruise	乘船游览，巡游
deliberately	故意地
denial	否认；拒绝，拒绝给予
figurative	（用词上）形象的，比喻的
firestorm	大爆发
handle	处理，操作，控制，应付，对待
increasingly	日益，愈加，越来越多地
majority	多数，大多数；票数差距，超过的票数
memo	备忘录
normally	通常地；正常地
notify	通知，告知，报告
occupancy	占有，使用，居住
option	选择（的自由）；选项；可选择的办法
original	原先的，最初的，最早的；新创的
overprice	将……标价过高，索价过高
payable	应付的，可付的
pervasive	无处不在的；遍布的；充斥各处的
policy	政策，方针；策略
protest	声明；抗议；拒付

recommend	劝告，建议；推荐，介绍
refrigerator	冰箱，冷藏库
remove	移走；排除；开除
representative	代表，代理人
respond	回答；回报；响应；作出反应
reverse	取消；撤销；推翻；（使）翻转废除
revise	修订，修改，修正
scheming	惯搞阴谋的；诡计多端的；狡诈的
sensor	传感器，灵敏元件
significant	重要的，有意义的；意味深长的
slip	滑，滑倒；偷偷/悄悄地塞给，塞入
spokeswoman	女发言人，女代言人
statement	声明，陈述，总述
suspicious	猜疑的，可疑的，表示怀疑的
transaction	处理，办理；（一笔）交易；（一项）事务
transition	过渡；转变；变迁
trap	陷进；圈套；（对付人的）计谋，陷阱
typically	代表性地，典型地，作为特色地
value	估价，重视，尊重
vast	极大的，大量的，巨额的

Phrases

a candy bar	一块糖
additional fee	额外费用
a vast majority of	绝大多数
express check-out	快速结账
goodie-box	糖果盒
late check-out	延迟退房
zero balance	零余额；偿清款项
accuse sb. of	指责、谴责某人……

be stuck in	掐住，卡住，动弹不得
be reserved for	留作，(专)供……之用
get to the point	抓住重点，进入正题
pull a fast one	欺骗
waste no opportunity	利用一切机会
at full-service	提供全方位服务

Part 4　Writing 写作技巧

Note
便笺

Note for Saying Good-bye

May 8, 2020

Dear Richard,

　　I'm leaving for home by air at six this evening. It is a pity that I can't see you to say goodbye before leaving. I have enjoyed my stay here. Thank you very much for your hospitality and the trouble you have taken on my behalf. Please remember me to your parents.

　　Yours,

　　Bill

Transmitting a Telephone Message

11:00 a.m.

Chen Wei,

　　Miss Wu, your classmate, has just rung up, saying that she has arrived this morning by train and is staying at Ramada Hotel (Room 509). She wants you to go there to discuss the schedule tomorrow and ring her back as soon as possible.

　　Liu Yang

Note Asking for Leave

April 10

Dear Professor Brown,

  I am very sorry that I shall be unable to attend class today owing to a bad cold and high fever. I'm enclosing a certificate from my doctor who said I must stay in bed for two days. I ask you for two days' sick leave. I shall be much obliged if I can get your permission.

  Yours respectfully,

  Wang Xiaopeng

  Encl: a certificate from my doctor

Receipt

December 15, 2020

  Received from Mr. Hill the following things: One typewriter, one tape-recorder, and 2,000 yuan only.

  Bruce

便笺常用句型

  (1) Will you please excuse my absence for...?

  我因……不能到场,望见谅。

  (2) I shall be much obliged if you grant me my application for three days' leave of absence.

  如果您能批准我三天的假期,我将感激不尽。

  (3) Because of..., I'm unable to come.

  因为……,我不能前来。

  (4) Please come this afternoon if possible.

  如果可能,今天下午务请光临。

  (5) I hope there will be no much trouble to you if...

  如果……我希望这不至于给您带来太多的麻烦。

  (6) received/ borrowed from...

收到/借到……

Writing Practice

a. Fill in the following reservation letter by translating the Chinese in the brackets.

Mr. Liang,

Mr. Zhou, _____ （你不在时，中国旅行社的导游来过电话）. It seemed that he wanted to talk with you about something really urgent. _____ （他要你尽快给他办公室回电话）.

Yours sincerely,

Han Meimei

b. Suppose you are Henry: you have received a telegram saying that your grandfather is seriously ill. You want to go home to see him. Please write a note to ask director White for a business leave of a week beginning on April 9.

Part 5 Vocabulary Expansion 词汇扩展

advanced deposit	押金
b & b (bed and breakfast)	提供床位和早餐
bell captain	服务生领班
bell desk	服务台（服务生领班和服务生待命的柜台）
bookkeeper	记账员
change money	换钱
charge ... to	记账
coin	硬币
customer affairs manager	客服经理
discount	折扣
guest folios	客人账户
heating fee	供暖费
hotel rates	房价
hotel register	旅馆登记簿

identification card	身份证
in the name of	在（某人）的名下，以（某人）的名义
information desk	问讯处
invoice	发票
key card	钥匙卡
left-luggage office	行李暂存处
luggage depository	行李存放处
night porter on duty	夜间值班的行李搬运服务生
overdue	过期的
overpay	多付（钱款）
payment in full	全额付款
peak rate	高峰时间价
porter	门童，门房，行李员
prepayment	预收款
procedure fee	手续费
refund	退款
room card	房卡
room service	客房服务
self check-out	自助结账
settle the account	结账
tariff	价目表
the means of settlement	结算方式
trunk	大衣箱

Unit 10 Dealing With Special Problems 应对特殊问题

Unit 10

Dealing With Special Problems 应对特殊问题

Learning objectives 学习目标

After learning this unit, you should
- acquire the knowledge about how to deal with problems and emergencies;
- organize the basic words and expressions about illness and disasters;
- learn some knowledge about travelers' checks;
- find ways to improve your writing skills in claim letters;
- be familiar with first aid techniques.

 Part 1 Background knowledge 背景知识

During the journey, a variety of special problems and emergencies may occur

133

sometimes. Therefore, it's necessary for a travel agency to have the abilities to handle such problems.

Types of Problems and Emergencies 问题与突发事件类型

food poisoning	食物中毒
typhoon	台风
hurricane	飓风
tsunami	海啸
elevator incident	电梯故障
physical assault	人身伤害
terrorist attack	恐怖袭击
equipment breakdown	设备故障
earthquake	地震
fire	火灾
losing the way	迷路
street fight	打架斗殴
explosion	爆炸
getting sick	生病
losing properties	遗失财物
traffic accident	交通事故
flood	洪水
gas leakage	燃气泄漏
power failure	停电
kidnapping	绑架
hijacking	劫持

 Part 2　Speaking 对话训练

Dialogue 1

A Careless Guest

(Scene: A careless guest, Mr. Bell has locked himself out of the hotel room. Now

Unit 10 Dealing With Special Problems 应对特殊问题

he is asking a clerk for help.)

A: I've locked myself out of the room. May I borrow a duplicate key?

B: Don't worry, Mr. Bell. I'll open the door for you.

(She opens the door with a duplicate key.)

A: Thank you very much. Sometimes I'm quite absent-minded.

B: It doesn't matter, Mr. Bell. Is there anything else I can do for you?

A: Ah, I'm afraid there's something wrong with the TV. The picture is wobbly.

B: I'm sorry. May I have a look?

A: Here it is.

B: (Tries to fix it, but in vain.) I'll send for an electrician from the maintenance department. We can have it repaired. Please wait just a few minutes, Mr. Bell.

(She leaves the room. Ten minutes later, there is a knock on the door.)

Electrician (E): May I come in?

A: (Opens the door) How do you do?

E: How do you do? The TV set is not working well. Is that right, Mr. Bell?

A: No, it isn't.

E: Let me have a look.

(The Electrician finishes the repairing and checks other electric facilities in the room.)

E: Mr. Bell, everything is OK now.

A: How efficient! Thanks a lot.

(Taking out some tips.) This is for you.

E: Oh, no. We won't accept tips, but thank you, anyway. We wish you a nice stay with us, Mr. Bell.

Notes

1. duplicate key   备用钥匙
2. absent-minded   心不在焉的
3. wobbly   摇摆不定的
4. electrician   电工，电学家
5. maintenance   维修，保养
6. facility   设备工具（常用复数）
7. efficient   有效率的

Dialogue 2

Claiming for Damage and Loss

(Scene: A careless guest (G) has thrown a cigarette end on the bedcover and burnt a hole in the bedcover and the blanket. The housekeeper (H) is talking to the guest.)

H: Good morning, Mr. Smith.

G: Good morning.

H: I am the housekeeper. May I know what happened here?

G: Sure. I met some friends in the room last evening. We smoked and talked a lot. When I was going to bed, I suddenly found there was a cigarette end in the bed. The bedcover and the blanket were burnt.

H: I'm sorry to hear that. Please let me take a look first.

G: OK, here they are.

H: Oh, I am really sorry to tell you that they are badly damaged. These are all quite new and have been used no more than a week.

G: I do apologize for what I have done.

H: Well, I am afraid we have to charge them to your account.

G: May I know how much they are?

H: About 350 yuan.

G: That's about two nights' room price.

H: If a fire started, you couldn't imagine the outcome.

G: That's true. I'll never forget the lesson. By the way, what are you going to do with the bedcover and blanket?

H: Don't worry, sir. I'll ask the chambermaid to give you a new bedcover and a blanket for this evening.

G: And the damaged ones?

H: Now, they are all your belongings. You may take them with you.

G: Oh, I don't think my wife will like to see them. She always advises me to give up smoking.

1. cigarette   香烟
2. bedcover   床罩

3. hole　　　　　　　　洞，破洞

4. damage　　　　　　　损坏，毁坏

 Part 3　Reading 快速阅读

Passage 1

Travelers' Checks

When traveling abroad, it's always wise to carry your money in travelers' checks because checks are protected against loss or theft. If your checks are lost or stolen, the issuing authority will refund your money.

Not only are they safe, they are also convenient. They are available in different denominations and different currencies and they can be cashed at most banks throughout the world. Most shops, hotels and restaurants also accept them.

To obtain travelers' checks, you usually go to your bank. They can be paid for in cash or debited to your account. Large amounts, however, must be ordered in advance.

For the safety and convenience of travelers' checks, you are charged two commissions. An insurance commission when you buy them and an encashment commission when you cash them.

They are very easy to use. When you collect them you sign each check once. The cashier enters the amount in your passport. When you cash you sign each check again. The cashier will usually ask to see your passport again too.

It is advisable to make a note of the serial numbers and denominations of your

checks in case they are lost or stolen. Keep this separate from the checks.

Vocabulary

account	计算，账目，说明
advisable	可取的，明智的
authority	权威，威信，权威人士；权利
cash	兑现，现金
charge	装满，控诉，收费
commission	委托，佣金
convenient	便利的
currency	流通，货币
debit	记入借方
denomination	命名，(货币等之) 单位或类别
encashment	付现，兑现
insurance	保险，保单，保险费
issue	发行（钞票等）；出版（书等）
serial	连续的
theft	偷，行窃，偷窃行为

Phrases

traveler's check	旅行支票
make a note of	记下，记录
pay for	付款，支付
protect against	防御，保护
separate from	分开，分离
in advance	预先，提前
in case	以免，万一
in cash	用现金
throughout the world	全世界

Passage 2

An Accident

Jack is the manager of a 120-seat restaurant in a resort area in Hong Kong. As the dinner crowd starts to thin out one night, he hears a sound outside the door of his restaurant.

When he opens the door, he sees that a wife of one of his customers is sitting on the steps holding her ankle. The light beside this door isn't very bright, but he thinks he sees her husband rushing to the car. Jack asks if there's anything he can do to help and the woman tells him that her husband is taking her right to the emergency room to get her ankle checked out. She tells Jack that he'll be sure to get the hospital bill and more. Her husband pulls up alongside her, gets his wife in the car, and tells Jack, "you'll hear from me!"

As promised, the next day her husband drops off the hospital bill to Jack and threatens a lawsuit. Jack tells him that he doesn't understand, after all he did ask if he could help, and he explained that the door they used was not the proper exit for guests. It was an employee entrance and exit. At this point, the man tells Jack, "you'll hear from my lawyer."

Unit 10 Dealing With Special Problems 应对特殊问题

Vocabulary

alongside	在旁边
ankle	脚踝
exit	出口
lawsuit	诉讼（尤指非刑事案件）
lawyer	律师
resort	求助；诉诸；凭借；胜地
threaten	恐吓，威胁

Phrases

hospital bill	医疗费用清单
the emergency room	急诊室
check out	结账，检查
drop off	将某物送到某地
hear from	收到某人的信件、消息等
pull up	停止
thin out	减少

Part 4 Writing 写作技巧

A Claim Letter
索赔信

Claim for the Lost Baggage

Dear Mr. Stewart,

On May 2, I arrived on the flight 603 from Baltimore to St. Louis. However, the suitcase I checked at your counter prior to the flight never arrived in St. Louis and hasn't been found in the six weeks since. Nor have I been reimbursed for the value of the suitcase and its contents.

When it became apparent that my luggage was missing I reported it to your Miss Rachel at the baggage claim area in St. Louis. Before leaving the airport I filled out a report. I am enclosing a copy of that report with this registered letter. Also enclosed is a copy of the claim check I was issued in Baltimore, along with an itemized list of the contents of the suitcase and the approximate value.

I realize that your liability covers only the depreciated value of the missing items and not the cost of replacing them. Since the total amount of the claim is well under the 75% of passenger liability limit for baggage-loss claims on domestic flights, I see no point in further delay in processing the claim.

Yours truly,

Henry Lee

Claim for the Interference

Dear Mr. Paul,

On the weekend of June 3-5, three friends and I attended the Political Women's Seminar held in your hotel. We had a room reserved for two nights, but on one of those nights were able to get very little sleep.

On the second night there was a high school prom in the hotel. From midnight till 3:00 a.m., the teens were roaming the halls shouting, banging on doors and being as rowdy as they could. Our calls to the desk brought promises, but no action.

The next morning we went to the registration desk and asked for a refund for that night and were told that was impossible. Since we had paid for two nights in advance, we were stuck.

We understand these were unusual circumstances, Mr. Paul, but if you wish to continue to draw seminar groups to your hotel, some changes in policy must be made. If we do not receive a refund for that night we will make sure the political women no longer have their annual seminar in your hotel.

Yours truly,
Jane Smith

Writing Practice

Fill in the following claim letter by translating the Chinese into English in the brackets.

Dear Mr. Hobing,

In early April I sent a check for a ＄50 deposit for my son, Brad, to attend summer camp. Brad _____ (多年来一直盼着参加夏令营).

Two days ago he _____ (骑自行车出了事故). He broke his right wrist and sprained his left ankle and, needless to say, is in no shape to attend camp next week.

I am enclosing a note from Dr. Ted outlining the extent of Brad's injuries. I realize you've had a space reserved for him. But in view of his accident and my prompt notification, _____ (请退还50元押金,我们不胜感激).

Cordially yours,
Jack Han

Part 5 Vocabulary Expansion 词汇扩展

各种旅游常见病的症状描述

appendicitis	阑尾炎
arthritis	关节炎
abdominal pain	腹痛
allergic to	过敏
breathing difficulty	呼吸困难
cold	感冒

cut finger	割破手指
diarrhea	痢疾，腹泻
dizzy	头晕
flu	流感
fracture/ break	骨折
heat stroke	中暑
headache	头疼
high fever	高烧
hepatitis	肝炎
heart attack	心脏病
nose bleeding	流鼻血
pneumonia	肺炎
running nose	流鼻涕
sunburnt	晒伤
stomachache	胃疼
sore throat	嗓子疼
toothache	牙疼
ulcer	溃疡
vomit	呕吐

Test 1

I. Match the word or phrase on the left with the statement on the right.

1. overbooking _____   a. shelter, food, drink, and other services for travelers

2. check-in _____   b. making more money than is needed for expenses

3. profitable _____   c. a vacation area with recreational facilities

4. cashier _____   d. a statement of all transactions affecting the balance of a single account

5. bill _____   e. to give a job, equipment etc. to someone for a particular purpose

6. accommodation _____   f. making more reservations than there are rooms or space in a hotel

7. assign _____   g. record of what the customer must pay

8. resort _____   h. registration, or the time when guests are greeted and the records for the guests' services and charges are set up

9. complaint _____   i. a statement that something is wrong, a grievance

10. folio _____   j. an employee in the accounting office of a hotel who checks the accuracy of postings on the guest accounts

II. Match the following two groups of words and phrases.

1. front office department _____   a. 信用卡

2. single room _____   b. 门挂菜单

3. credit card _____   c. 国际长途直拨

4. emergency exit _____   d. 早餐券

5. door knob menu _____   e. 接线员

145

6. fitness center _____   f. 单间

7. operator _____   g. 健身中心

8. IDD _____   h. 安全出口

9. quilt _____   i. 前厅部

10. breakfast voucher _____   j. 被子

III. Fill in the spaces in the following sentences with the appropriate word or phrase from the texts.

> informs, log book, shift, occupancy, messages, check, courteously, arrival

1. Because hotels operate twenty-four hours a day, many jobs are scheduled on a morning, evening, or night-_____ basis.

2. Before beginning their shifts, Front Desk agents should _____ the log book for ongoing activities or possible problems.

3. The Front Desk _____ the housekeeping when a guest has checked out, so that the room can be prepared for the next guest.

4. Housekeeping notifies the Front Desk when a room is clean and ready for _____.

5. Prompt handling of mail and _____ is very important to registered guests.

6. They should respond _____ when helping guests with their local and long-distance telephone calls.

7. In most hotels, guest mail is stamped with the time of _____ and is held in the appropriate slot in the mail-and-message rack at the Front Desk.

8. Front Office employees communicate among themselves by using a Front Office _____.

IV. Cloze

> worth, with, up, found, thirsty, and, where, in, stop, at, selling, pushing

Passage 1

　　Snacks can be __1__ in every city and all over the city. The Chinese are inveterate (积习难改) snackers and the roadside stalls __2__ steamed savory (味美) buns and

146

other "fast food" have been __3__ business for a very long time. If you are __4__ you can have a beer from a corner beer shop, and __5__ the same time maybe try a small dish of sliced kidneys or a spring roll. If you are in the South, then it's __6__ having at least one meal in a dim sum (点心) restaurant. In the North you would go to a "small snack" restaurant. This is __7__ people meet, from mid-morning until mid-afternoon, to catch __8__ on the latest news or even to discuss business. These restaurants are usually large, noisy and friendly. In dim sum restaurants, waiters course around the room __9__ trolleys loaded down __10__ delicious bite-sized snacks, and you simply __11__ them and take your pick. In the North, more prosaically, you pick your snacks up at the counter. The food is normally quite light and non-greasy, __12__ usually steamed rather than fried.

Passage 2

BOT Investment

BOT (Build, Operate, Transfer), as a way of __13__, is still a new concept in China. It is also not long for BOT to gain importance in foreign countries. That is because this __14__ which embraces the three stages of BOT (Build, Operate, Transfer) is completed by a package __15__ so it has its own characteristic. BOT is mainly applicable to __16__ projects such as highway, underground railway, bridge, dock and power plant in a developing country or zone which is especially short of capital but is eager to __17__ on reform and opening to the outside world. It involves at the same time government, group in charge of preparation for project construction, construction contractor, banking and financing institutions, operation management company and others, thus forming nearly integral __18__ operation. Besides, in the whole BOT project, about ten contracts, big and small, need to be concluded with various parties. To carry out such complicated investment, one ring __19__ with another, can be both difficult and easy.

The risk in BOT should be __20__ by all parties, rather than being undertaken by one party. In the whole BOT project, the risk undertaken by the government is obviously the smallest, relative to the other parties. It is just because of this that the government is willing to adopt the BOT way of investment, assigning a private company to build and operate a large-scale capital construction, considering the serious __21__ in capital and the numerous infrastructures to be built. When the government decides to adopt the BOT way of investment on certain infrastructure project, the first thing to be done is legislation, to be followed by __22__ of license, looking for target of cooperation, conducting negotiation and then concluding contract. The risk of the government lies in issuing the license to a private project company with reliable strength to plan the whole BOT project, not making the mistake of "trusting the wrong person".

13. A. investment   B. operation   C. building   D. management
14. A. job   B. party   C. project   D. way
15. A. contract   B. arrangement   C. construction   D. program
16. A. infrastructure B. appliance   C. commercial   D. bank
17. A. begin   B. start   C. embark   D. undertake
18. A. conflicted   B. coordinated   C. match   D. share
19. A. attaching   B. coping   C. linking   D. cooperating
20. A. shared   B. designed   C. expended   D. exceeded
21. A. advantage   B. shortage   C. disadvantage   D. plenty
22. A. issue   B. issuance   C. booking   D. management

V. Reading comprehension

Restaurant services

There are mainly five kinds of restaurant services. They are guerdon service, silver service, plate service, buffet (self-catering) service and takeaway service. The first three kinds of services are sit-down services and a buffet service can be both a sit-down one and a stand-up one.

Take away service is usually associated with snack bars and fast food outlets. In guerdon service, the waiter must always be well-trained and skilled for he has to perform such things as filleting carving and cooking special dishes in front of the guest. In silver service, the food is prepared in the kitchen and brought to the guest's table on a silver tray. In plate service, the waiter takes the plated meal from the service hotplate and then put the plate on the guest's table. All that he has to do is to make sure that the correct lid is laid and the necessary accompaniments are available on the table. In buffet service, a guest picks his or her own tray and cutlery from one end of the service table and choose whatever dish he or she likes.

Two forms of meals are distinguished: a la carte and table d'hote. An a la carte meal is ordered course by course from a menu where each item has a separate price while a table d'hote meal has a fixed price for a complete meal or several courses.

1. Which of the following can be a stand-up service?

   A. Gueridon service.   B. Silver service.

   C. Plate service.   D. Buffet service.

2. Why is a take-away service usually associated with snack bars?

   A. The food in snack bar is easy to takeaway.

   B. People go there by cars.

   C. Snack bars can be found anywhere.

   D. Snack bars offer self-catering service.

3. What meal is it when you can order your dishes separately?

   A. Buffet.   B. a la carte.

   C. Table d'hote.   D. Plate service.

4. In the context of the passage, available means (   ).

   A. Necessary   B. Can be got

   C. Helpful   D. Served

5. In the context of the passage, distinguished means (   ).

   A. Well-known   B. Made out

   C. Separated   D. Different

VI. Translate the following sentences into English.

1. 稍等，我帮您结算账单。
2. 离开之前，还有什么需要我做的吗？
3. 你要大额还是小额钱币？
4. 打扰了，我是来收衣服的，请问您有要洗的衣服吗？
5. 我们可以在4小时内送回，但是要增收50%的费用。

Test 2

I. Match the word or phrase on the left with the statement on the right.

1. amenity _____   a. a sum of money that is given back to the guest

2. log book _____   b. a form with several parts that contains information about hotel guests and a place to record charges and money paid

3. posting _____   c. an official recorded or written record of something

4. switchboard _____   d. a piece of equipment for connecting and disconnecting telephone calls

5. due-outs _____   e. a hotel employee who does heavy housekeeping chores, especially in the public areas of the hotel

6. deposit _____   f. a room from which a guest is expected to check out on a given day who has not yet done so

7. houseman _____   g. a service or item offered to guests or placed in guest rooms for convenience and comfort and at no extra cost

8. issue form _____   h. an outlet where fast-food service is available

9. snack bar _____   i. a place where guests can have breakfast or a quick meal at a moderate price

10. cafeteria _____   j. a record of the date and quantity an item is dispensed, signed by the person who withdraws and the person who gives permission for the withdrawal

II. Match the following two groups of words and phrases.

1. foreign exchange _____   a. 夜班服务员

2. bellboy _____   b. 外汇兑换

3. collect call _____   c. 游泳衣

4. luggage rack _____   d. 行李架
5. overnight staff _____   e. 行李员
6. DND sign _____   f. 熨烫
7. bath mat _____   g. 婴儿床
8. ironing _____   h. 对方付费电话
9. baby cot _____   i. 地巾
10. swimming suit _____   j. 请勿打扰标志

III. Fill in the spaces in the following sentences with the appropriate word or phrase from the texts.

payment, transactions, cashing, financial, revenues, posted, accuracy, charges

1. Cashiers provide _____ services to the customers at the Front Desk, including receiving payment for bills, making change, and exchanging foreign currency.

2. The cashier may also be responsible for other guest banking service, such as check _____.

3. Front Office cashiers have to handle different methods of _____.

4. Some business guests request direct billing of the _____ to the company for which the guest works.

5. The cashiers receive payments from guests and enter the final _____ on electronic equipment at the Front Desk.

6. Prior to, or at the time of check-out, the cashiers must make sure that guest charges in the hotel are _____ to the proper accounts.

7. Night auditors examine Front Office accounting records for _____.

8. Auditors track room _____ and compare these against occupancy figures.

IV. Cloze

provide, for, location, supplies, reduces, unaware, where, cleaned, basement, successful, take, storage, changed, may, back, clean, ties, advisable, design, inconvenience

Most of the guests in a hotel are __1__ of the facilities in the __2__ of the house,

151

such as the linen room, the __3__ areas for extra furniture and equipment, and all the other parts of the hotel that __4__ comfort to the guests. The __5__ and __6__ of these facilities are an important aspect in a __7__ operation. To __8__ just one example, rooms must be __9__ and linens must be __10__ on a daily basis. If the linen storage room is located in the __11__ the elevator must be used to take the chambermaids and their carts to the floors __12__ they will work. This __13__ up the elevators and __14__ therefore __15__ the guests. It also __16__ the time during which the chambermaids can __17__ their assigned rooms. __18__ these reasons, it is __19__ to provide a storage area for housekeeping __20__ on each floor.

V. Reading comprehension

The art of growing dwarf trees, or "bonsai" as their Japanese creators call them, is increasing in popularity in the Untied States. Growing bonsai can make a fascinating hobby for anyone who enjoys plants and creating beautiful effects with them; elaborate equipment is not required to grow these lovely and tiny trees, but time, patience, and a sense of natural beauty are.

There are four important guidelines to follow in growing bonsai. First, one must be careful in choosing the type of tree. Not all species of trees can be made into bonsai, since the growing conditions are unusual. Varieties of pine with small needles and hardwood trunks are especially suitable.

Second, one must be careful in choosing the size of the container the bonsai will be in. This is necessary because the major growth of bonsai is kept confined to the tree's trunk and leaves, not its root system—a process quite unlike what is done with other plants.

The third thing the bonsai-grower must do is trim the roots and branches of the tree periodically. Unless this is done, the plants will not have the proper proportions and will look unnatural. The Japanese ideal for bonsai is to have trees which are just like normal trees in everything but size.

The last thing one must do is to be careful to keep the miniature trees well-watered. Because bonsai are grown in smaller-than-usual containers, they often need more water than ordinary houseplants do.

As one can see from the above, the art of bonsai-growing is one which requires a certain amount of time and effort. The satisfactions that growing bonsai brings can be great, however. Imagine a stately pine tree, 100 years old, standing two feet high; imagine having such a tree in your living room and passing it down through several generations of your family. That is actually what bonsai-growing is all about: establishing a tradition of beauty which lasts for years and years and is a symbol of the beauties of the natural world.

1. Bonsai are ( ).

    A. extremely popular in the United States

    B. trees which have been made to grow in miniature form

    C. a kind of natural art form originating in the U. S.

    D. very beautiful but not very long-lasting

2. Compared to other houseplants, bonsai often require ( ) than one might expect.

    A. less light   B. more water   C. a large container   D. less care

3. What does the ideal bonsai look like?

    A. It has abnormally large leaves.   B. It has an unusually thick trunk.

    C. It has many more branches.   D. It is not mentioned in the passage.

4. What is the implied meaning of "a certain amount of time and effort" (last paragraph)?

    A. More time and effort than ordinary houseplants do.

    B. A definite and exact amount of time and effort.

    C. More time and effort than most people can expend.

    D. A constantly changing amount of time and effort.

5. Which of the following would be the most appropriate title for this passage?

    A. Japanese Art Forms.   B. Bonsai—A Marriage of Art and Nature.

    C. The Problems of Growing Bonsai.   D. Four Ways to Grow Bonsai.

VI. Translate the following sentences into English.

1. 请您填写登记表。
2. 请您先付 1 000 元作订金。
3. 请您准备好行李，我们把您安排到另外的房间。
4. 多长时间和费用是多少？
5. 您希望我们如何布置会场？

Test 3

I. Match the word or phrase on the left with the statement on the right.

1. lodging _____
2. deposit _____
3. premise _____
4. baby-sitting _____
5. memo _____
6. occupancy rate _____
7. information _____
8. housekeeper director _____
9. rating _____
10. night auditor _____

a. the building and land a hotel uses
b. a level on a scale that shows how good a hotel is
c. a place to stay
d. taking care of infants or children on a temporary basis while their parents are away or busy
e. the percentage of rooms or beds occupied in a hotel during a given period
f. an amount of money that is paid into a bank account
g. an accounting term for a person who enters charges on the appropriate financial record
h. a collection of information kept at the Front Desk for Front Desk agents to use in responding to guest requests
i. a short official note to another person in the same company or organization
j. a person who supervises cleaning and making up rooms for hotel guests

II. Match the following two groups of words and phrases.

1. deposit _____
2. general switchboard _____
3. receipt _____

a. 前台接待
b. 跑步机
c. 吸尘器

4. peep hole _____   d. 维修服务

5. vacuum _____   e. 总机

6. bathrobe _____   f. 干洗服务

7. dry-clean _____   g. 猫眼

8. maintenance service _____   h. 押金

9. receptionist _____   i. 发票

10. treadmill _____   j. 浴袍

III. Fill in the spaces in the following sentences with the appropriate word or phrase.

> amount, deliver, Laundry, supplied, chambermaids, guestrooms, report, activities

1. Your guests will not patronize your hotel unless your _____ are well decorated with fresh air and spotless and polished furniture.

2. The actual work of cleaning and caring for the guest rooms is performed by the _____.

3. The chambermaids are expected to _____ any signs of damage or wear and tear that may make repairs necessary.

4. Chambermaids have a limited _____ of contact with the guests.

5. Guests frequently ask chambermaids for items that are _____ by the housekeeping department, such as matchbooks, irons, special pillows, or pitchers of cold water.

6. In some hotels, the chambermaids pick up and _____ clothing for the laundry and valet service.

7. _____ and valet service must provide quick and efficient service to guests who need clothes washed, cleaned, or pressed.

8. A housekeeping staff must coordinate his _____ closely with the Front Desk.

IV. Cloze

> receive, travel, interfere, convenience, pick, located, reception, cash, advice, operation, information, pigeonholes（存放文件的框架）, appropriate, includes, transportation, sections, messages, arrangements, counter, area

For the __1__ of the guests, the Front Office is almost always __2__ near the hotel's main entrance. In a large hotel, it is divided into __3__. One section is the __4__ desk, where the guests register or check in. The second section is the __5__ where the guests __6__ up their keys, mails and __7__. This part of the __8__ has a rack behind it with __9__ for each guest room in the hotel. The key to each room is kept in the __10__ pigeonhole. The third section is an __11__ desk, where the guests can ask for information or make local travel __12__. This area often __13__ a mail-box. The fourth section is the cashier's desk. The cashiers not only __14__ payment from the guests, but also __15__ checks, make change, and exchange foreign currency. Some hotels also offer a __16__ desk, where the guests may get __17__ or help with their __18__ plans. This service, however, is often located in another part of the lobby so that it may not __19__ with the efficient __20__ of the Front Office.

V. Reading comprehension

Hotel Operation

In order to see that all the activities of the hotel run smoothly and efficiently, the manager carries out routine spot checks, often on a daily basis, of different aspects of the hotel's operation. He also deals with unusual problems as they occur. In a large hotel, he coordinates the work of the department heads who supervise their respective departments. The manager's working relationship with these people has a lot to do with the smooth functioning of the hotel. Hiring and training are two other vital responsibilities of the manager. The personality, experience, and technical know-how of every employee in the hotel are matters of importance in a business where courtesy are one of the major services. The references given by job applicants are carefully checked and during the job interview, the applicant's initial behavior is observed.

A watchful eye must be kept on their performance after they have been hired. Continuing in-house training programs are necessary in order to maintain the standards of the establishment.

1. According to this passage, the hotel manager (   ).

   A. usually works in his office

   B. should have good relations with department heads

   C. should check every department every day

D. deals with unusual problems every day

2. The overall responsibility of the hotel manager is (   ).

   A. to ensure the smooth operation of the hotel

   B. to ensure a good working atmosphere

   C. to solve unusual problems

   D. to check different aspects of the hotel's operation

3. What are the important aspects mentioned here in a staff-hiring program?

   A. The personality of the staff.

   B. The work experience of the staff.

   C. The technical know-how.

   D. All of the above.

4. Before a person is hired by a hotel, (   ).

   A. he will receive training provided by that hotel

   B. he is checked by the hotel

   C. he should send in letters of reference

   D. he should maintain good standards

5. When a person has been hired by the hotel, (   ).

   A. he will definitely receive training

   B. he should expect that his work is supervised

   C. he should expect to go to an interview

   D. he should keep a watchful eye

VI. Translate the following sentences into English.

1. 您打算待多久？

2. 今天美元的汇率是多少？

3. 稍等，我帮您结算账单。

4. 我们会把费用加到您房间的账单上。

Test 4

I. Match the word or phrase on the left with the statement on the right.

1. coffee shop _____
2. menu _____
3. pantry _____
4. furnishings _____
5. niche _____
6. guaranteed _____
7. room status _____
8. voucher _____
9. profit margin _____
10. function reservation _____

a. the description of the room about its occupancy and its condition

b. the furniture and other things in the room, such as curtains, baths, etc.

c. a list of food and beverage items

d. a place where dishes, china and glassware are stored, some even have facilities for warming the food

e. small restaurants mainly concentrating on cakes, sandwiches, coffee and tea, and no alcoholic beverages

f. an opportunity to sell a particular product to a particular group of people

g. a large party or ceremonial event, especially for an important or official occasion

h. a record of a charge transaction in the hotel

i. a reservation that assures the guest that a room will be held until check-out time of the day following the day of arrival

j. the difference between the cost of producing something and the price you sell it at

II. Match the following two groups of words and phrases.

1. exchange memo _____   a. 电梯
2. baggage tag _____   b. 电水壶
3. elevator _____   c. 会议
4. check out _____   d. 托婴服务
5. personal check _____   e. 电吹风
6. hair dryer _____   f. 针线包
7. conference _____   g. 行李牌
8. baby sitting service _____   h. 结账退房
9. water boiler _____   i. 兑换水单
10. sewing bag _____   j. 个人支票

III. Fill in the spaces in the following sentences with the appropriate word or phrase from the texts.

authorized, update, formality, establishment, registration, reservation, efficient, assignment

1. The main function of Front Desk agents is to complete the _____ process.
2. The registration record contains information that Front Desk agents use in the _____ of a room and rate for each guest.
3. The Front Desk agents should check the expiration date of the credit card and obtain an _____ code during the registration process.
4. Upon guest arrival, Front Desk agents should warmly greet guests and inquire about the guests' _____ status, usually by requesting the confirmation notice.
5. When agents have to _____ the registration form, they input new data directly on the computer keyboard.
6. One was already assured of the job and his interview was a mere _____.
7. A good manager is both competent and _____.
8. The manager is the host who offers the hospitality of his _____ to his guests.

IV. Cloze

incurred, expense, affirmative, cash, works, fall, contact, addition, settle, expedite, pose, departing, like, exchange, verify, takes, required, employees, nevertheless, beverage

The cashiers are the accounting office __1__ who have direct __2__ with the guests. In __3__ to settling accounts, they also make change, __4__ traveler's checks or regular bank checks, and __5__ foreign currencies. Posting on the room accounts are kept up-to-date in order to __6__ the check-out procedure. __7__ the check-in procedure, it __8__ only a few moments, when the system __9__ efficiently, for a guest to __10__ his bill. __11__, the cashiers usually ask the __12__ guests if they have __13__ any last-minute charges for the telephone or for food and __14__ service. If the answer is __15__, the cashier must __16__ the charge before presenting the final bill. The cashiers are often __17__ to ask if the guest has turned in his key. Lost keys are an __18__ for the hotel; more seriously, they __19__ a threat to security if they __20__ into the wrong hands.

V. Reading comprehension

As we know, it is very important that a hotel pays attention to the training of its staff, as there exist many weak parts in its various departments. Staff training must have a purpose, which is defined when a hotel considers its training needs, and in turn based on job descriptions and job specifications.

A job description should give details of the performance that is required for a particular job, and job specification should give information about the behavior, knowledge and skills that are expected of an employee who works in it.

When all of this has been collected, it is possible to make a training specification. This specifies what the training department must teach for the successful performance of the job, and also the best methods to use in the training period.

There are many different training methods, and there are advantages and disadvantages of all of them. Successful training programs depend on an understanding of the difference between learning about skills and training in using them. It is frequently said that learning about skills takes place "off the job" in the classroom, but training in using these skills takes place "on the job", by means of such activities as practice in the workshop. It is always difficult to evaluate the costs and savings of a training program. The success of such a program depends not only on the methods used but also on the quality of the staff who do the training. A hotel can often check on savings in time and cost by examining the work performed by the staff who have completed a training program. The evaluation of management training is much more complex than that.

1. To be successful in our training program, we must understand the difference between (   ).

    A. a job description and a job specification

    B. what is taught and how it is taught

    C. learning about skills and training in using them

    D. the saving in time and the saving in cost

2. The success of a training program depends on (   ).

    A. the places where the training takes place

    B. the correct evaluation of the costs and savings of the program

    C. the performance of the workers and technicians receiving training

    D. the training methods and the quality of the training staff

3. What does a training specification specify?

    A. The performance required for a certain job.

    B. The behavior, knowledge, and skills expected of an employee.

    C. The training contents and methods used.

    D. The costs and savings of the program.

4. According to the passage, which of the following is true?

    A. All staff members need training now and then.

    B. Training in using skills and learning about skills usually happen at the same time.

    C. It is easier to evaluate the training of staff than to evaluate management training.

    D. A training specification is only based on the information collected from job description.

5. Which of the following would be the best title of this passage?

    A. Staff Training.   B. Management Training.

    C. A Successful Training.   D. Value of Staff Training.

VI. Translate the following sentences into English.

1. 你不需要等很久，下一个就是你了。
2. 请问会议什么时候举行？
3. 我刚刚扫完地，我可以继续（打扫）吗？
4. 我马上派人上来修理。
5. 我可以刷一下您的信用卡吗？

Test 5

I. Match the word or phrase on the left with the statement on the right.

1. early-makeup _____   a. a hotel employee who carries baggage and does other errands for the guests

2. follow-up _____   b. an employee specializing in assisting guests with their individual needs, whether in-hotel or off-premises

3. portion _____   c. one of many telephone lines in a hotel which all have different numbers

4. bellman _____   d. a room for which a guest has reserved an early check-in time or requested a cleaning as soon as possible

5. forecasting _____   e. a department that provides food and beverage service for special events

6. extension _____   f. food and beverage service delivered to the guest rooms of a hotel

7. room service _____   g. a kind of hotel providing parking facilities for cars

8. catering _____   h. short-term planning that approximates the number of rooms available for sales on any future date

9. concierges _____   i. something that is done to make sure that earlier actions have been successful or effective

10. motel _____   j. the specific amount of each food served to the customer

II. Match the following two groups of words and phrases.

1. tissues holder _____   a. 购物长廊

2. room service _____   b. 深水泳池

3. french cuisine _____   c. 纸巾盒
4. shopping arcade _____   d. 大堂
5. baggage checks _____   e. 送餐服务
6. lobby _____   f. 美式早餐
7. swimmer's pool _____   g. 法式菜肴
8. American breakfast _____ h. 枕头
9. pillow _____   i. 行李票

III. Fill in the spaces in the following sentences with the appropriate word or phrase from the texts.

> hospitality, resident, clientele, caters, offers, feature, facilities, available

1. All hotels do not serve the same _____; that is, the same kind of guests.
2. Each means of transportation has resulted in the growth of corresponding accommodations _____.
3. Old-fashioned inns did provide food and shelter for both men and horses and therefore became a symbol for _____.
4. The larger and more luxurious the hotel, the greater the variety of jobs that it _____.
5. The airplane made many more places _____ for development as resorts, including places that were quite isolated.
6. A _____ hotel provides accommodations for people who do not wish to keep house themselves.
7. The holiday company _____ more for the elderly.
8. This policy is a key _____ of our long-term corporate planning.

IV. Cloze

> install, wake-up, scheduled, answers, automatic, unauthorized, status, restocking, accounting, discrepancies

Often, hotels __1__ telephone systems with sophisticated (复杂，高级) features for reasons other than just cost effectiveness. Examples of these features include automatic call dispensing (分配) systems, telephone/room status systems and call detection (监测) equipment.

In many cases, automatic call dispensing is limited to __2__ services. The operator enters the room number and time for each wake-up call into the computer. At the __3__ time, a telephone call is automatically placed to the guest's room. Once the guest __4__ the call, the computer may activate a synthesized voice that reports the current time, temperature, and weather conditions. Another variation on __5__ call dispensing allows the hotel to call rooms in case of an emergency or to call all guests with a specific group to remind them of a meeting.

Telephone/room status systems can assist with room management and prohibit the __6__ use of telephones in vacant rooms. Housekeeping or room service employees can use guestroom telephones to enter data concerning room service charges (for example, what was consumed from an in-door bar), maintenance information, or current room __7__ information. These features lower payroll costs and help ensure a more efficient in-room bar __8__ system.

Call detection equipment works with the hotel's telephone equipment and call __9__ systems. Call detection equipment can pinpoint the exact moment a telephone call is connected. This helps improve billing accuracy and reduces guest account __10__ since only answered calls will be billed.

V. Reading comprehension

Passage 1

Using a public telephone may well be one of the minor irritations of life, demanding patience, determination and a strong possibility of failure, together on occasion with considerable unpopularity.

The hopeful caller (shall we call him George?) waits till six o'clock in the evening to take advantage of the so-called 'cheap rates' for a long-distance call. The telephone box, with two broken panes of glass in the side, stands at the junction of two main roads with buses, lorries and cars roaring past. It is pouring with rain as George joins a queue of four depressed-looking people. Time passes slowly and seems to come to a standstill while the person immediately before George carries on an endless conversation, pausing only to insert another coin every minute or so.

Eventually the receiver is replaced and the caller leaves the box. George enters and picks up one of the directories inside, only to discover that someone unknown has torn out the very page he needs. Nothing for but to dial Directory Enquiries, wait patiently for a reply (while someone outside bangs repeatedly on the door) and finally note down the number given.

At last George can go ahead with his call. Just as he is starting to dial, however, the door opens and an unpleasant-looking face peers in with the demand, "Can't you hurry up?" Ignoring such barbarity, George continues to dial and his unwanted companions withdraw. At last he hears the burr-burr of the ringing tone, immediately followed by rapid pips demanding his money but he is last located them, he dials again: the pips are repeated and he hastily inserts the coins. A cold voice informs him, "Grand Hotel, Chalfont Wells." "I've an urgent message for a Mr. Smith who is a guest in your hotel. Could you put me through to him? I'm afraid I don't know his room number."

The response appears less than enthusiastic and a long silence follows. Gorge inserts more coins. Then the voice informs him, "I've been trying to locate Mr. Smith but the hall porter reports having seen him leave about a minute ago."

Breathing heavily, George replaces the receiver, just as the knocking on the door starts again.

1. The main intention of the passage is to provide ( ).

    A. instructions about how to use a public call box

    B. advice about how to deal with public telephone problems

    C. criticism of possible annoyances in using a public telephone

    D. an account of possible annoyances in using a public telephone

2. Which of the following calls are you unlikely to make at the 'cheap rates' referred to?

    A. to discuss your account in a bank in Scotland

    B. to have a chat with an elderly relation

    C. to ask about a friend in hospital who has just had an operation

    D. to express Christmas greetings to cousins in Australia

3. George can at least be thankful that ( ).

A. the call box is in a convenient position

B. the telephone itself is working

C. he can use the directory in the box to find the number

D. he is able to give his message to the hotel receptionist

4. What are George's feelings when he completes his call?

A. He has some difficulty in controlling his annoyance.

B. He is very disappointed at missing his friend.

C. He is annoyed with himself for being so stupid.

D. He is depressed at the thought of having to try again to get through.

Passage 2

The General Manager

As in any business, there must be one person responsible for the overall operation. That person is the general manager, sometimes, particularly in the larger hotels, called the managing director.

In the past, possibly into the 1930s, the hotel manager was primarily a genial host, personally greeting the guests and seeing to it that they were properly cared for. But as the banks (through bankruptcies and foreclosures), corporations, conglomerates, and other business organizations began acquiring hotels, this image began to disappear.

The first concern of executives and stockholders of these companies was that the property shows a profit. As a result, a new type of innkeeper emerged, and today the successful general manager is a highly trained person, capable of directing a complex business enterprise.

Running a hotel is a full-time, 24-hours-a-day, seven-days-a-week operation. The hotel is never closed—there can be no time off, no holidays. Someone representing management, and some members of the operating staff, must be on duty every hour and every day of the year. No broad policy could possibly cope with the many diverse situations that occur daily in any given hotel.

The general manager is the person responsible for defining and interpreting the policies established by top management. In addition, the successful manager must implement and improve them and, on occasion may be forced to completely disregard them. To perform these duties properly requires a working knowledge of all phases of hotel operation. No one can properly give or explain an order without some idea of what is involved. The quickest and easiest way for an executive to lose the respect of the employees is to give instructions without understanding their implications or the amount of time necessary to carry them out. In fact, we believe it is impossible to properly and intelligently supervise anyone without having at least a general idea of that person's duties and responsibilities.

5. What's a hotel manager's responsibility?

   A. Overall operation.

   B. Administrative affairs.

   C. Several main departments.

   D. Greeting the guests.

6. A general manager should (   ).

   A. Define the policies

   B. Interpret the policies and implement the policies

   C. Be capable of directing a complex business enterprise

   D. Implement the policies

7. There are always persons in charge working in the hotel round the clock because (   ).

   A. Staffs are working in the hotel

   B. They want to greet the guests

   C. They want to know the general ideas of the staffs

   D. There are always things that happen unexpectedly

8. A successful manager is the person who can implement and improve (   ).

   A. hotel facilities

   B. policies established by top management

   C. surrounding environment

   D. relations between hotel and guests

9. In the context of the passage, a full-time means (   ).

   A. 12-hours-a-day

   B. 24-hours-a-day

   C. seven-days-a-week

D. 24-hours-a-day & seven-days-a-week

VI. Translate the following sentences into English.

1. 恐怕单间都订完了，换个大床间怎么样？

2. 请稍等，我帮你接线到2032。

3. 您的账单总计1 500元，包括15%的服务费。

4. 先生，请问什么时间比较方便？

5. 您的房间朝南，拥有美丽的海景。

参考文献

[1] 何加红. 酒店管理英语. 北京：首都经济贸易中心出版社，2012.

[2] 宿荣江. 酒店管理英语. 北京：首都经济贸易中心出版社，2011.

[3] 司爱侠，陈红美. 饭店酒店管理英语. 天津：南开大学出版社，2008.

[4] 范广丽，袁立辉. 酒店管理英语听说教程. 北京：对外经济贸易大学出版社，2012.

[5] 纪可. 酒店管理英语. 北京：国防工业出版社，2006.

[6] 鲁阿凤，司爱侠，王凤元. 饭店酒店管理专业英语实用教程. 北京：清华大学出版社，2012.

[7] 匡仲潇. 星级酒店常用英语大全. 北京：化学工业出版社，2013.

[8] 滕悦然. 餐饮服务常用英语口语大全. 北京：化学工业出版社，2014.

[9] 宿荣江. 酒店实用英语. 北京：中国人民大学出版社，2013.

[10] 邸丽霞，姜涛. 酒店服务英语. 北京：中国人民大学出版社，2013.

[11] 宁毅. 酒店服务英语. 重庆：重庆大学出版社，2008.

[12] 姜涛，王书芳. 酒店英语实训手册. 北京：中国人民大学出版社，2014.

[13] 谌桂君，董姝. 酒店服务英语. 北京：北京理工大学出版社，2011.

[14] 盛丹丹. 酒店英语. 北京：中国水利水电出版社，2010.

[15] 曹玉泉，房玉靖. 酒店英语实训教学参考书. 北京：对外经济贸易大学出版社，2011.

[16] 黄培希. 酒店英语辅导用书. 北京：对外经济贸易大学出版社，2013.

[17] 李雪. 酒店职员英语口语大全. 3 版. 北京：机械工业出版社，2015.

[18] 周春艳，王国栋. 英语口语大全：酒店英语. 西安：西北工业大学出版社，2010.

[19] 王向宁. 酒店情境英语：下. 北京：北京大学出版社，2015.

[20] 李洪涛. 英语口语话题系列：酒店英语口语话题王. 天津：天津科技翻译出版公司，2012.

[21] 沈婵，方志仁. 酒店服务业英语口语. 北京：中国石化出版社有限公司，2011.

[22] 范雪菲. 酒店英语这句话：应急最好用. 北京：中国宇航出版社，2014.

[23] 成应翠，韩伟. 终极酒店服务口语一本就够. 北京：中国水利水电出版社，2014.

[24] 陈的非，刘朝晖. 饭店实用英语. 北京：机械工业出版社，2008.

[25] 郭淑梅. 酒店管理实务英语. 2版. 北京：高等教育出版社，2015.

[26] 赵晓芳，杨昉，范若楠. 星级酒店管理实务系列：星级酒店常用英语. 广州：广东经济出版社有限公司，2012.

[27] 刘丽. 酒店服务英语. 上海：格致出版社，2013.

[28] 王丽华，王金茹，李艳. 酒店服务英语. 北京：北京理工大学出版社，2012.

[29] 潘桂君. 酒店服务英语. 2版. 北京：中国商业出版社，2007.

[30] 胡扬政. 现代酒店服务英语. 2版. 北京：清华大学出版社，2013.

[31] 谢钰. 国际酒店服务英语. 北京：中国人民大学出版社，2012.

[32] 韩敏. 酒店服务英语. 北京：中国铁道出版社，2013.

[33] 陈丹. 酒店饭店英语口语实例大全. 北京：中国宇航出版社，2009.

[34] 胡朝慧. 酒店英语. 北京：北京大学出版社，2011.

[35] 王琳. 酒店英语. 天津：南开大学出版社，2012.

[36] 麦榕. 酒店英语. 北京：旅游教育出版社，2013.

[37] 吴云，吴文婷，钱嘉颖. 酒店英语. 北京：中国旅游出版社，2014.

[38] 尚宏. 酒店英语. 郑州：郑州大学出版社，2012.

[39] 王迎新. 酒店英语. 2版. 北京：中国林业出版社，2011.